Nashville Metro

Nashville Metro

THE POLITICS OF CITY-COUNTY CONSOLIDATION

Brett W. Hawkins

Foreword by Judge David Briley

VANDERBILT UNIVERSITY PRESS

Nashville, Tennessee

Library of Congress Cataloging-in-Publication Data

Names: Hawkins, Brett W., author.
Title: Nashville metro : the politics of city-county consolidation / Brett
 W. Hawkins ; foreword by Judge David Briley.
Description: Nashville, Tennessee : Vanderbilt University Press, [2025] |
 Series: Vintage Vanderbilt; vol. 9 | Includes bibliographical references
 and index.
Identifiers: LCCN 2024056861 (print) | LCCN 2024056862 (ebook) | ISBN
 9780826507426 (paperback) | ISBN 9780826507433 (epub) | ISBN
 9780826507440 (pdf)
Subjects: LCSH: Nashville Metropolitan Area (Tenn.)--Politics and
 government.
Classification: LCC JS451.T38 N3 2025 (print) | LCC JS451.T38 (ebook) |
 DDC 352.076855--dc23/eng/20241129
LC record available at https://lccn.loc.gov/2024056861
LC ebook record available at https://lccn.loc.gov/2024056862

FOR GLORIA

CONTENTS

RE-INTRODUCTION

I T has been more than sixty years since the voters of Davidson County decided to merge the governments of the City of Nashville and Davidson County. Over those six decades, the mythology surrounding consolidation has grown that emphasizes how Nashville subsequently differed from the rest of the South—less conflict over race, a more utilitarian approach of regulation, pro-growth policies. Simultaneously, the mythology around Diane Nash and Mayor Ben West's 1962 encounter has developed in the same manner—Mayor West acknowledged the immorality of the segregated lunch counters when pressed—how different from the rest of the South.[1] I submit that these mythologies are part and parcel of what has become Nashville's "immoderately moderate" approach to governing.

Nashville Metro: The Politics of City-County Consolidation largely falls in line in line with (or perhaps created) that mythology. Its introduction points to the following questions: "Why have metropolitan area voters been so reluctant to approve major reorganization proposals? Who supports governmental reorganization, or integration, in metropolitan areas, and who opposes it? What sort of voter attitudes underlie opposition and support? What kinds of interests, individuals, and groups get involved?" It clearly addresses the environment in which consolidation took place from an academic, neutral, utilitarian perspective consistent with the dominant thinking of the time. In this context the author briefly raises

---

1 Perhaps more emphasis should be placed on Diane Nash's audacious confrontation of Mayor West and less on Mayor West's concession.

issues of race in the context of larger discussions of the politics surrounding the difficulties (generally and specifically) of altering the form
of municipal government. It does not look at consolidation in a primarily race conscious way.

Like most myths, Nashville's mythology of consolidation contains an
element of truth. The last six decades have seen unparalleled economic
growth and prosperity. Likewise, the expanded geography of metropolitan government mitigated the consequences of white flight in the 1970s
and 1980s, resulting in today's multiracial municipality. Currently, the
tax base has grown so much that it supports the State generally. Indeed,
by many measures, consolidation has been nothing short of miraculous
and we owe the voters and leaders who made it happen a debt.

Nevertheless, a retrospective assessment of the politics of consolidation should, in this observer's opinion, warrant more emphasis on
the racial consequences of the decision. Notably, the nonpartisan elections of municipal officials did not result in a Black person's elevation
to a countywide position from 1962 to 1999. This failure contrasts to the
growing power of the Black vote in the City of Nashville leading up to
consolidation.[2] Only after the imposition of term limits in 1999 did Metropolitan Nashville elect a Black candidate to a countywide municipal
position. We should assess the struggle of the Black community that took
place over those four decades. I submit that Howard Gentry's ultimate
election as vice mayor was the result of much struggle and delayed aspirations which might not have been needed or occurred without consolidation. Looking back at consolidation with this fact in mind would, in
my opinion, add depth to the mythology of consolidation by appropri-
ately emphasizing the sacrifice of the Black community in the resulting
prosperity of Nashville.

I do not suggest this further assessment of consolidation as a criticism of the consolidators—instead I suggest it to offer more fullness to
the consolidation mythology. Within the context of the suburbanization
of America and the contemporaneous civil rights movement, consolidation did result in many positive developments for Nashville, and the mythology about Nashville's exceptionalism is certainly warranted in many

2 This growing power was subject to minimization through the City's
   annexation of suburban areas of Davidson County.

respects. However, a mythology that omits the sacrifice of Nashville's Black community fails to fully acknowledge those responsible for Nashville's post-consolidation success. This failure can easily be addressed.

Finally, as the descendent of one of the principle advocates of consolidation, I would offer that a full, fair assessment of *all* the consequences of consolidation will extend Nashville's exceptional past. And while conversations about race are always fraught, it is especially important to acknowledge the consequences to Nashville's Black community that supported consolidation.

Nashville Metro

INTRODUCTION

THE problems of governing the nation's metropolitan areas
have drawn more and more attention in recent years. This
is reflected both in the growing volume of literature on
the subject and the increasing interest in ways to reform the governmental structure of such areas.

But in spite of extensive interest in reform few major structural
changes have occurred when a vote was required. From 1950 to
1961 there were eight failures in eleven attempts, the only successes being two consolidations in Virginia[1] and the achievement
of a metropolitan county in the Miami, Florida area.[2]

Why have metropolitan area voters been so reluctant to approve major reorganization proposals? Who supports governmental reorganization, or integration,[3] in metropolitan areas, and

1. In 1952, the Town of Phoebus, the City of Hampton, and Elizabeth
City County consolidated into the City of Hampton. In 1958 the cities of
Warwick and Newport News consolidated into the City of Newport News.
(In 1952, Warwick, then a county, had incorporated as a city of the first
class.) There is reason to believe that government reorganizations in
Virginia are not really comparable with those elsewhere. See David G.
Temple's forthcoming work on consolidation in Tidewater, Virginia, and
Brett W. Hawkins's forthcoming work on the Virginia system of urban
government. Basically, the hypothesis set forth in these books is that
because of Virginia's long and continuing tradition of local government
reform, popular attachment to the structural status quo is relatively loose
in Virginia.

2. See Chapter Four for a review of the record of failures.

3. So called because it involves the process of bringing together, or unit-
ing, the governments of the metropolitan area. The concept of govern-

who opposes it? What sort of voter attitudes underlie opposition and support? What kinds of interests, individuals, and groups get involved?

In controversies over metropolitan integration, as in nearly all political controversies, interest groups discern that the outcome will somehow affect them, and thus they tend to behave in various determinate ways. In every such controversy, moreover, a decision is made, even if only a tacit decision to preserve the status quo. How are such decisions reached?

These are the fundamental questions toward which this book is directed. It is not designed to analyze metropolitan problems and tell how to solve them. Rather, this study will focus on the actual state of things politically.

Our major purpose is to contribute to a body of systematic knowledge about opposition to and support for governmental integration in metropolitan areas. More specifically, this study is designed to contribute to an understanding of the conditions under which integration proposals are likely to succeed and the conditions under which they are likely to fail. A second important purpose is to examine in detail one instance of the process of metropolitan integration, for as Scott Greer has pointed out this process has not been studied extensively.[4]

SCOPE

On June 28, 1962, four years after they had turned down a similar proposal, the voters of Nashville and Davidson County, Tennessee, approved a charter consolidating the city and the

---

mental integration in metropolitan areas is based on the view that local communities (subareas) in metropolitan areas are interdependent, and that integrative governments are needed to formulate and execute area-wide policies in which all share a common interest. Since "integrative governments" involve major governmental "reorganization" these terms are used interchangeably in this book.

4. "Dilemmas of Action Research on the 'Metropolitan Problem,'" in *Community Political Systems*, ed. Morris Janowitz (Glencoe, Illinois: The Free Press, 1961), pp. 202–205.

county. As the Buffalo *Courier Express* noted sometime later, this was a rare occurrence:

> Seldom if ever has a city government of any consequence in the United States gone out of business. It is happening in Nashville, Tennessee, however. The city's governmental shop is being closed up. . . .[5]

The Buffalo paper might have added that technically the county's governmental shop was also closed up. The result, in any case, has been a great deal of interest in Nashville's "Metro." How did it happen? How was a consolidation accomplished in the Nashville area when so many less thoroughgoing proposals had been defeated elsewhere?

This book attempts to answer the question of how the Nashville consolidation was accomplished; it also tests a number of explanatory hypotheses of voter support and opposition derived from relevant political science literature. In addition, the alignment of interest groups in Nashville is examined and compared with relevant propositions about interest-group behavior.

Chapter Two surveys the literature on metropolitan government and politics and considers what some see as gaps in that literature. Chapter Three describes the general Nashville setting, with special emphasis on political and governmental conditions. Chapter Four presents the hypotheses about voter attitudes and interest-group alignments that are tested in this study. The fifth and sixth chapters deal with the background to the 1962 Metro referendum, with special emphasis on the unsuccessful referendum of 1958.

Chapter Seven discusses the 1962 charter commission and the resulting charter. The eighth and ninth chapters consider in the light of the Nashville data the problem of explaining opposition and support for governmental integration. Chapter Eight focuses specifically on the alignment and activities of interest groups, and Chapter Nine focuses on voter attitudes.

The last chapter presents the author's general conclusions.

5. Buffalo *Courier Express*, August 12, 1962.

2

POLITICAL SCIENCE AND "THE METROPOLITAN PROBLEM"

N OT all of the enormous outpouring of literature on
metropolitan areas has been of interest to political
scientists. But much of it has. For the political scientist
undertaking metropolitan area research, this literature may be
divided into two main currents: one is the reformist stream with
its emphasis on good government, structure, functions, and
efficiency; the second might be called sociological because of
its emphasis on community power structure, political influence,
and opinion leadership. Although not excluding the latter, this
chapter concentrates on the reformist stream. It deals specifically
with the reformist view of "what's wrong" with the present structure of metropolitan government, with proposed solutions to that
problem, and with the outlook of those political scientists who
dissent from the reformist position.

One of the common themes to be found in reformist literature
is the alleged defectiveness of the existing structure of local government in metropolitan areas. Basically, the allegation is that
there are "too many governments" in such areas and that this
"multiplicity" results in inefficient administration, overlapping
and duplication of governmental functions, and in an inability
to cope with areawide problems. Such defects grow continually
worse, moreover, as urban and metropolitan growth proceeds.

Thus reformers view as pathological the existence of numerous
governmental units in the metropolitan area, and for this reason

they tend to concentrate on achieving the integration of metropolitan area governments.[1]

In his now classic *Metropolitan Government,* written more than twenty years ago, Victor Jones summarized the reformist view in these words:

> Disintegrated local government in metropolitan areas results in unequalized services, in a disparity between need and fiscal ability to meet the need, and in a dispersion and dissipation of political control of the development of social, economic and political institutions. . . . everywhere—in Europe, as well as in America—the problem of providing services for the entire metropolitan community and of financing and controlling its local government is conditioned by its disintegration.[2]

More specifically, reformers see various consequences of "disintegrated" government in metropolitan areas. The first of these is described as the inequities in financing local public services. Governmental services in metropolitan areas tend to be unequally distributed, depending upon the the financial resources of the various units of government. In many instances the heaviest service needs occur in the areas with the least financial capacity, that is, in the low-income areas.[3] In some cases, however, unequal

1. Following is a partial list of reformist literature: John C. Bollens (ed.), *Exploring the Metropolitan Community* (Berkeley: University of California Press, 1961); Editors of *Fortune, The Exploding Metropolis* (Garden City, New York; Doubleday, 1958); Webb Fiser, *Mastery of the Metropolis* (Englewood Cliffs, New Jersey: Prentice Hall, 1962); American Academy of Arts and Sciences, "The Future Metropolis," in *Daedalus,* XC, No. 1 (Winter, 1961); Luther H. Gulick, *The Metropolitan Problem and American Ideas* (New York: Knopf, 1962); Victor Jones, "Local Government Organization in Metropolitan Areas," in *The Future of Cities and Urban Redevelopment,* ed. Coleman Woodbury (Chicago: University of Chicago Press, 1953); W. A. Robson (ed.), *Great Cities of the World: Their Government, Politics, and Planning* (London: Allen and Unwin, 1954).

2. *Metropolitan Government* (Chicago: University of Chicago Press, 1942), p. 52.

3. Victor Jones, "Local Government Organization in Metropolitan Areas," in *The Future of Cities and Urban Redevelopment,* ed. Coleman Woodbury (Chicago: University of Chicago Press, 1953), pp. 520–524.

services are more the result of community preferences than of tax-base differentials, as, for example, in suburbs which prefer not to provide public fire and police protection.

Another major concern is how a multitude of local governments of various sizes can cope with areawide problems. A major argument here is that local communities in metropolitan areas are mutually interdependent and that integrative governments are therefore needed to formulate and execute areawide policies in which all have a stake.[4] From an administrative standpoint, moreover, fragmented government is held to be illogical and inefficient, whether the problem is transit, water, sewers, health, or planning. "In the absence of a single integrated metropolitan government with authority to guide the progress of the whole urban region, unified policy formation and execution is an impossibility."[5]

A final problem is said to be the existence of barriers to democratic control of government in metropolitan areas. Part of the problem stems from the very multiplicity of governmental units and the inability of even the very interested citizen to cope with the resulting patchwork. Perhaps a more important dimension of this problem is the inability of the citizen to hold responsible any one official or unit of government. "Which official or unit of government is to receive the credit or blame for over-all metropolitan goods or ills? Will the bewildered citizen blame the county, the central city, the suburban cities, or the many special districts for sluggish commuter traffic?"[6] To many reformers this is the most serious problem of all.

---

4. On the subject of the interdependence of metropolitan subareas see R. D. McKenzie, *The Metropolitan Community* (New York: McGraw Hill, 1933) and Edward C. Banfield and James Q. Wilson, *City Politics* (Cambridge: Joint Center for Urban Studies of M.I.T. and Harvard University, 1963), esp. Chap. 4.

5. Daniel R. Grant and H. C. Nixon, *State and Local Government in America* (Boston: Allyn and Bacon, 1963), p. 341.

6. *Ibid.*

PROPOSED INTEGRATIVE DEVICES

Nor have metropolitan reformers been reluctant to offer "solutions to the metropolitan problem." On the contrary, they have put forward a great many inventive "solutions" in recent years. Some of them contemplate major changes in existing governmental institutions and some only minor changes. It is important that the reader be generally familiar with those devices contemplating major changes, for it is just such devices that the country's metropolitan voters have been reluctant to approve (perhaps less so in the case of annexation), despite fervent appeals in the name of good government or efficient administration.

Briefly, the reforms that contemplate the greatest change[7] in existing governmental institutions are geographical consolidation, annexation, city-county separation, and the metropolitan county and "federation."

The consolidation of existing governments is perhaps the favorite device of reformers because it reduces the number of governmental units. In practice, however, consolidation has been hard to achieve, although there are isolated examples of city-county consolidation,[8] intermunicipal consolidation,[9] and even intercounty consolidation.[10] Some of the obstacles to achieving consolidation are legal ones. Some state constitutions do not

7. Devices involving less disruption of existing governments include formal and informal agreements between governments, the creation of special districts to perform one or more areawide functions, voluntary metropolitan associations made up of public officials from area governments and designed to promote a common approach to common problems, and the consolidation of specific governmental functions.

8. Baton Rouge and East Baton Rouge Parish in 1947; Hampton, Phoebus, and Elizabeth City County, Virginia, in 1952; Nashville and Davidson County in 1962; South Norfolk and Norfolk County, Virginia, in 1963; and Virginia Beach and Princess Anne County, also in 1963. In the last century such consolidations took place in the Boston, Philadelphia, New Orleans, and New York areas.

9. Manchester and Richmond, Virginia, in 1910; Waynesboro and Basic City, Virginia, in 1920; and Warwick and Newport News, Virginia, in 1958.

10. Campbell, Milton, and Fulton Counties, Georgia, in 1931 and 1932.

permit consolidation at all, and among those that do, enabling legislation, often difficult to pass, is commonly required. Many states, moreover, require separate petitioning, and separate majorities, in the geographical areas involved. Additional reasons for the failure of proposed consolidations include unfavorable voter attitudes, reluctant governmental officials, and the failure of largely upper-status reform groups to win over the average voter. All of these reasons are examined more closely below.

The annexation of county territory by a municipality is advo- cated by reformers because it enables the municipality to absorb its urban spill-over. Annexation thereby inhibits the formation of new municipalities in urban fringe areas. At least this is the hope. Annexation sometimes has the opposite effect in practice; that is, it brings about defensive incorporations in fringe areas (to avoid being annexed). Annexation only inhibits the formation of new towns and cities when municipal incorporation is discour- aged at the same time that annexation is encouraged. In Tennes- see, it is worth noting, incorporation was greatly discouraged in 1957.[11]

Annexation is seldom easy to achieve. Once again, statutory restrictions are partly responsible. State annexation laws typically require the consent of a majority of the residents in the area to be annexed. Many states even require separate majorities in both the area to be annexed and in the annexing municipality.[12] The

11. Within two miles of a city of 5,000 to 99,999 inhabitants and 5 miles of a city of 100,000 inhabitants or more, any proposed incorporation is held in abeyance for 15 months. If during that time the central city annexes as much as 20 per cent of the area, or 35 per cent of the population, of the territory to be incorporated, the petition for incorporation is rendered null and void.

12. The states of Virginia, Texas, Tennessee and North Carolina permit their municipalities to exercise much more initiative in annexation pro- ceedings than do other states. See R. G. Dixon, Jr., and J. R. Kerstetter, *Adjusting Municipal Boundaries: The Law and Practice in 48 States* (Chi- cago: American Municipal Association, 1959). On the general subject of annexation Frank S. Sengstock *Annexation: A Solution to the Municipal Area Problem* (Ann Arbor: Legislative Research Center, University of

annexation of incorporated territory, moreover, is forbidden, except in a few states by special act of the legislature. This alone has rendered annexation virtually impossible in many of the larger and older metropolitan areas, for in such areas the central cities are often surrounded by incorporated communities.

City-county separation is intended to divide urban and rural populations so that each may have the services it desires and is willing to pay for.[13] In this century, city-county separation has fallen into almost total disuse, except in Virginia where any municipality, upon reaching a population of five thousand, may (the action is wholly voluntary) separate from the surrounding county and become a "city-county" performing both municipal and county functions.

Many states do not provide for city-county separation at all, but even those that do run into the practical problem that it is no longer easy to separate urban and rural populations. The county area outside today's city is often densely populated throughout and contains a wide scattering of residences, rather than a compact agglomeration close by the central city.

City-county separation is no solution in any case to the "problem of too many governments," for it does not reduce the number of governmental units. Also, separation is an act of withdrawal and therefore a step away from metropolitan integration. In Virginia, however, the cities of Hampton, Virginia Beach, South Norfolk, and Newport News consolidated with counties after first separating from them.

The metropolitan, or "urban," or "municipalized," county involves giving municipal-like powers to the county. Several counties in New York State, Virginia, and especially in California have

Michigan Law School, 1960). For a systematic treatment, see Thomas R. Dye, "Urban Political Integration: Conditions Associated with Annexation in American Cities," *Midwest Journal of Political Science,* VIII, No. 4 (November 1964).

13. Roscoe C. Martin, *Metropolis in Transition* (Washington, D. C.: Housing and Home Finance Agency, 1963), p. 9.

undergone such an expansion of their powers, in many cases with a reorganization of their traditional, decentralized county administrations as well.

Reformers have shown in recent years a great deal of interest in using the county as a unit of areawide government in metropolitan areas, partly because it already exists and partly because the piecemeal addition of municipal-like powers is politically feasible in many areas.[14] But attempting to make greater use of the county presents serious problems. In the first place, about one third of the nation's metropolitan areas extend over more than one county, rendering impossible their governing by a single county. Another problem is that restrictive state laws, constitutional provisions, and judicial attitudes usually strait-jacket county governments. It is not uncommon to find the county treated primarily as an "administrative arm" of the state with no important role to play in local self-government.

There are nevertheless some notable examples of municipalized metropolitan counties. Dade County (Miami), Florida, is probably the best-known example, although several California counties are also well known.[15] Dade County operates under a home-rule charter[16] with a manager form of government. The county's governing body consists of eleven members: five elected at large, five from districts, and one from the City of Miami. Responsibility has been given to the county for such areawide functions as transportation, fire and police protection, housing and urban renewal, zoning, and sewerage. Those functions not delegated to Dade County are exercised by the several municipal-

14. Victor Jones, for example, has argued for greater use of the county. See Coleman Woodbury (ed.), *The Future of Cities and Urban Redevelopment* (Chicago: University of Chicago Press, 1953), pp. 592, 593. See also the yearly articles in the *Municipal Year Book,* published by the International City Managers' Association, on the growth of county powers in the United States.

15. Los Angeles and San Bernardino counties in particular.

16. The charter was approved by the voters in 1957. See Edward R. Sofen, *The Miami Metropolitan Experiment* (Bloomington, Indiana: Indiana University Press, 1963).

ities, but the county is authorized to take over such functions if the municipality fails to meet certain standards set by the county.

It can readily be seen that the Dade County system is a kind of two-tier government. This system is sometimes called the federation or borough plan because it involves the division of governmental functions between an areawide layer of government and a local layer of government.

Besides Dade County, the other best-known example of this system is Toronto, Ontario, Canada. First established in 1954, Toronto's federal system was put into effect not by a vote of the people but by fiat of the Ontario Provincial Parliament.[17] Under the Toronto system, the existing county was abolished and replaced by a new entity called the "Municipality of Metropolitan Toronto." Responsibility was delegated to the latter for such areawide functions as housing, education, arterial highways, parks, water supply, sewerage, and planning. A 25-member governing body was created, consisting of 12 members from Toronto, one from each of the other 12 municipalities in the area,[18] and a chairman selected by the metropolitan council.

A similar system was established in 1960 in Winnipeg, Manitoba.

The federation plan has never been popularly approved in the United States except in Miami where the existing county was used to provide areawide government. Federation has been voted down in Oakland, Pittsburgh, St. Louis, San Francisco, Boston, and Cleveland. Part of the problem, once again, is the legal situation. State laws typically require separate majorities in all or most of the governments to be federated, and because federation diminishes the powers of existing local government it has a low political feasibility.

17. See John C. Grumm, *Metropolitan Area Governments; The Toronto Experience* (Lawrence: University of Kansas Publications, Governmental Research Series No. 19), and Frank Smallwood, *Metro Toronto: A Decade Later* (Toronto: Bureau of Municipal Research, 1963).

18. Actually, the council chairmen from the twelve municipalities sit on the metropolitan council.

DISSENT FROM THE REFORMIST POSITION

As indicated at the beginning of this chapter, the reformist position has not been free from criticism within the field of political science, and the criticism has actually increased in the past few years. Scott Greer, Charles R. Adrian, and Vincent Ostrom have all questioned the allegedly a priori assumptions of the metropolitan reformers.[19] Greer has also charged that the very definition of the subject of reformist literature, "the metropolitan problem," "indicates the presence of value assumptions at the outset of the enterprise; and research projects in this field have usually been intellectually oriented toward the improvement of the cities through changes in governmental structure."[20]

As early as 1958 Norton E. Long offered a number of criticisms of what he called the "save our cities" ideology.[21] Long's questions included the following: Is the reform movement simply the latest in a long line of rather naive urban panaceas, including nonpartisan elections, the short ballot, the model charter, the separation of politics and administration (or the banishing of "politics" altogether), and the general tendency to define good local government as technically proficient administration?

Other political scientists have charged that reformers overlook the fact that metropolitan integration implies the elimination of "grassroots" governments and that many Americans are firm believers in the small-government, "grass-roots" idea. They further argue that the grass-roots idea has been institutionalized and made legitimate in the existing (fragmented) governmental pat-

19. Greer, "Dilemmas of Action Research on the Metropolitan Problem," in *Community Political Systems*, ed. Morris Janowitz (Glencoe, Illinois: The Free Press, 1961), p. 188; Adrian, "Metropology: Folklore and Field Research," *Public Administration Review*, XXI, No. 3 (Summer, 1961), 148–157; Vincent Ostrom *et al.*, "The Urbanization of Government in Metropolitan Areas," *American Political Science Review*, LV, No. 4 (December, 1961), 831–842.

20. Greer, *op. cit.*, p. 188.

21. "Recent Theories and Problems of Local Government," *Public Policy*, ed. Carl J. Friedrich and Seymour E. Harris (Cambridge: Harvard Graduate School of Public Administration, 1958), pp. 285–295.

terns of the nation's metropolitan areas, thus constituting a form-idable obstacle to governmental integration.

Adrian has outlined some of the more specific "assumptions" of the reformers in singularly unsympathetic fashion.[22] We do not know, of course, whether the reformers actually hold the beliefs Adrian imputes to them; we are concerned solely with enumerating the items in his indictment:

That the core city must expand or die. Adrian states that this argument is a favorite of persons who have a financial stake in expansion—editors, chambers of commerce, downtown merchants, and city managers.[23]

That efficiency and economy are the highest political values held by American homeowners. Adrian contends that

> Leaders of metropolitan studies are likely to assume that efficiency of administration and economy in budgeting are the things that would be most preferred by residents—if only "politicians" didn't get in the way with selfish desires to preserve jobs and personal empires. Those who make this claim sometimes exclaim in wonder and horror, "Why there are sixty-seven different fire departments in the metropolitan areas."[24]

Adrian has also said that

> the reformers tend to forget that the symbols—efficiency, a bigger and better Zilchville, and the like—that they respond to with such enthusiasm ring no bells for the *hoi polloi . . . representativeness* of government and access to the decision maker are likely to be more important considerations for the typical citizen than are questions of efficiency and economy.[25]

That professional administration—which the core city has and the metropolitan-area government would have—is preferable to amateur administration. Adrian asks, "Preferable to whom? To many no doubt. But the typical citizen is ambivalent in his atti-

---

22. Adrian, *op. cit.,* pp. 149–152.
23. *Ibid.,* pp. 149, 150. Adrian should perhaps have added freelancing political scientists to this list.
24. *Ibid.,* p. 150.
25. Adrian, *Governing Urban America* (New York: McGraw Hill, 1961), p. 290.

tude. He wants a government of friends and neighbors, but he wants one that will deliver pure water to the tap."[26]

That a metropolitan-area government would save the taxpayers some money. Adrian suggests that the taxpayer would perhaps get more for his tax dollar, but not enough money could actually be saved by this method to make more than a dent in today's huge municipal budgets. Besides, metropolitan government would probably seek to raise service levels in the long run.

Thus the critics of reformist literature frequently argue that such literature is prematurely prescriptive and does not reflect the existing state of things politically, even though it may well reflect the existing state of local administration and of local public services. The critics complain that there has been little systematic research into voter attitudes for and against reorganization, how the reorganization process tends to work, and who the proponents and opponents of change are. This is what is meant by "the existing state of things politically." In the words of Greer, questions of this sort are "logically prior to the normative questions of bringing about desirable changes however determined." Many studies, he adds, make premature application of social science.[27]

It is, of course, partly in response to such complaints that this study was undertaken.

26. Adrian, "Metropology: Folklore and Field Research," p. 151.
27. Greer, *op. cit.*, p. 204.

3

NASHVILLE: THE SETTING

N ASHVILLE, the capital city of Tennessee, is located approximately in the center of the state, in Davidson County. The city's "Standard Metropolitan Statistical Area" (533 square miles) is defined by the United States Bureau of the Census as "coterminous", or coextensive, with the county. In 1960 the population of Davidson County was 399,743. In 1950 it was 321,758, and in 1940 it was 257,267. Table 1 shows this growth in terms of central city and the county outside.[1]

TABLE I

Population of Nashville Standard Metropolitan Statistical Area,
By Central City and County Outside: 1900–1960

Year	Nashville	Davidson County Outside
1900	80,865	41,950
1910	110,364	39,114
1920	118,342	49,473
1930	153,866	68,988
1940	167,402	89,865
1950	174,307	147,451
1960	170,874[a]	228,869

Source: Bertil Hanson, *A Report on Politics in Nashville* (Cambridge: Joint Center for Urban Studies of M.I.T. and Harvard University, 1960), Chap. I, p. 1.

a. Including 4,587 persons annexed in 1959. The legality of this annexation, however, had not been settled by the courts at the time of the 1960 census. At that time the city occupied 23.3 square miles.

1. Bertil Hanson, *A Report on Politics in Nashville* (Cambridge: Joint Center for Urban Studies of MIT and Harvard University, 1960). This chapter draws extensively from this work.

The pattern of growth indicated by these figures is consistent with the national pattern—that is, diminishing growth in the central city, even decline, and a mushrooming of the county area outside.

The largest cluster of population in the area is contained within the boundaries of the old City of Nashville; in fact the 1960 population of the old city was considerably more than the 170,874 reported by the Census Bureau because of the annexation in April, 1960, of an estimated 82,000 persons and 42 square miles. The total thus exceeded 250,000. There are, however, other important communities and clusters of population in the metropolitan area. These include the following census divisions of the county: Inglewood, Donelson, Madison, Old Hickory, Woodmont–Green Hills–Glendale, West Meade–Hillwood, Nashville Southeast, and Nashville South; and the incorporated communities of Berry Hill, Belle Meade, Oak Hill, Forest Hills, Goodlettsville, and Lakewood (formerly Dupontonia). (See map, "Nashville Urbanized Area," opposite, and Table II, p. 147 of the section entitled "Additional Tables.")

The county census divisions and communities south and southwest of the city generally represent centers of considerable wealth. Belle Meade and Oak Hill are especially affluent, and they are also the stronghold of many of the so-called "old families" of the area. Donelson, Madison, and Inglewood also contain numerous higher-income families, but by no means as many in proportion as the area stretching from West Meade to Crieve Hall. The Madison, Maplewood, Inglewood, Nashville Southeast, and Woodbine–Radnor–Glencliff areas contain mostly middle- to lower-income groups. Haynes Heights is an area that is rapidly filling with Negroes.

The City of Nashville contains relatively few neighborhoods comparable in wealth with the areas southwest of the city. Only a few parts of the old Fourth Ward, chiefly on or near West End Avenue, are similar in income.

As for its racial characteristics, the City of Nashville was 38.1 per cent nonwhite prior to the annexation of a large piece of county territory in 1960. The 82,512 persons annexed in that year were only 6.2 per cent nonwhite, however. Upon the final court settlement of this large annexation, the City of Nashville contained an estimated 253,386 people, 27.6 per cent of which were nonwhite. In 1940 the percentage of nonwhites in Nashville was 28.0; in 1950 it was 31.4.

Negroes are concentrated in North Nashville, lower East Nashville, and in a broad strip running through the downtown area in South Nashville. In many districts where they are in a majority, however, Negroes have failed to register in as high percentages as whites and are thus outnumbered on the lists of registered voters.

THE ECONOMY

Nashville is primarily a commercial rather than an industrial city, although it does contain some important industries, among them the Ford glass plant, Du Pont, Genesco, Gates Rubber, and Avco. But Nashville specializes in banking and insurance. Its Union Street, which fairly bristles with banks, investment houses, and loan associations, is often called the "Wall Street of the Central South" and in 1960 represented total bank deposits amounting to some 700 million dollars. Nashville's per capita buying income is reportedly 33 per cent above the regional average.[2] The city is also the home of two large insurance companies—the National Life and Accident Insurance Company and the Life and Casualty Company of Tennessee.

Government service also plays an important part in the city's economy. Nashville contains numerous municipal, county, state, and national agencies.

Local students of Nashville's politics point out that until quite recently the very nature of the area's economy was a hotly con-

2. *Ibid.*, Chap. 1, p. 9.

a. Source: U. S. Bureau of the Census, *United States Census of Population: 1960. Tennessee,* Vol. I.

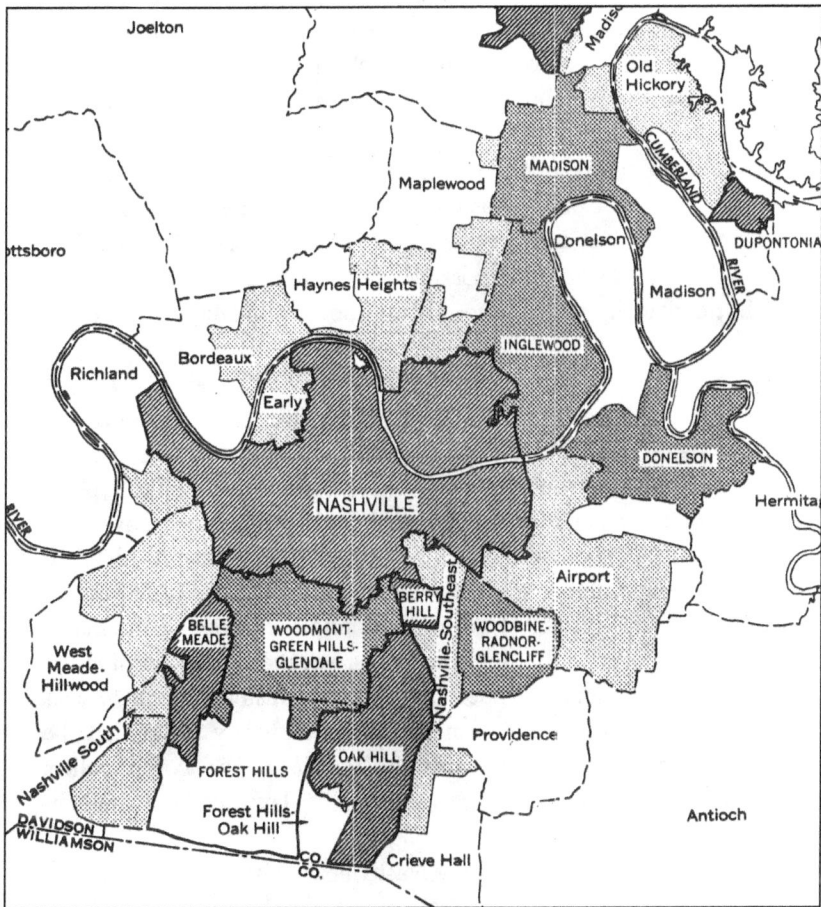

Detail of downtown Nashville and the surrounding neighborhoods.

tested issue. A good many affluent Nashvillians strenuously opposed industrialization and regarded it as a serious threat to the
existing order—an order from which they greatly benefited.

In recent years, however, Nashville has undergone a substantial
transformation in its generally "conservative" physiognomy.
Many observers place considerable credit (or blame) for this
transformation on the Nashville *Tennessean* whose publishers, the
Silliman Evans family, came to Tennessee as Texas New Dealers
in the late 1930s. Other possible contributing factors are Vanderbilt University and the more liberal policies of Mayor Ben West.

THE GOVERNMENTAL SETTING

The government of the City of Nashville before consolidation
was based on a charter that underwent substantial change in 1947.
In that year a strong mayor-council form was adopted to replace
the mixed form under which the city had operated for many years.

The charter of the old City of Nashville was a lengthy, detailed
document, totaling some eleven thousand words. It prescribed
not only the system of government and the duties of the major
officials but also the duties, salaries, vacations, and pensions of
the lesser officials. Under the charter, Nashville's mayor was
elected to a four-year term and given authority to appoint the
heads of the twelve departments: finance, public works, police,
fire, welfare, water, health, assessment, law, aviation, maintenance, and purchases.

The Council of the City of Nashville consisted of 21 members,
20 of whom were elected from single-member districts and one
of whom, the Vice-Mayor was elected at large and presided over
council meetings. The city also operated some two dozen boards
and commissions. Most appointments to these bodies were made
by the mayor with the consent of the council.

The man who has the distinction of having been the last mayor
of Nashville is Ben West (elected for the first time in 1951). An
attorney, West is considered a vigorous administrator and is widely
known among American municipal officials, having been presi-

dent of the American Municipal Association at one time. West
is also an ardent champion of urban causes, most notably state
legislative reapportionment (he was one of the plaintiffs in the
historic case of *Baker* v. *Carr),* urban renewal, and federal and
state aid to cities.

During his administration Mayor West dominated the city
government. Roughly two thirds of the City Council was said to
"be reluctant to speak or vote in a manner that might embarrass
Mayor West."[3] One of the principal means of maintaining such
support was reputedly by the use of patronage.[4] It is reported
that West handled patronage personally. Indeed, he allegedly
made a "practice of warmly greeting every prospective employee,
civil service or not, and asking questions about the location of
the man's home, members of his family, their ages and voting
habits."[5] In contrast to the City, Davidson County (prior to consolidation) had not experienced a change in its governmental
form for a very long time. In fact its governmental machinery
operated within the framework that existed more than a century
ago. In addition, the county governing body (called the quarterly
court) had not been adequately reapportioned since 1950 and
seriously overrepresented rural areas.

The basic structure consisted of the traditional Tennessee
"county court–county judge" arrangement. The county court included 55 magistrates elected from 16 civil districts, one of which
(the first civil district) coincided with the limits of the City of
Nashville.

The Davidson County Court was not only the county's legislative body but also constituted a major part of its administrative
machinery. Through its committee system and through the selection of numerous boards and commissions, the County Court
exercised many functions usually regarded as executive in nature.

The County Judge was only nominally the counterpart of the

3. *Ibid.,* Chap. 2, p. 4.
4. *Ibid.*
5. *Ibid.,* p. 5.

city's mayor, moreover. He could not appoint persons to county boards or commissions, nor could he exercise authority over the county trustee (in Tennessee a combination tax collector and county treasurer), tax assessor, sheriff, or attorney general, all of whom were independently elected. The County Judge did, however, enjoy paramount authority over county finances, including budgeting and accounting. Partly as a consequence of this authority, and partly owing to his position as the central figure in county government, the County Judge could wield considerable influence. But he was not chief administrator in the sense that the mayor was. Also, it was difficult to separate administrative from legislative responsibilities in the government unit of which he was the central figure.

At the time of the 1962 Metro vote, the County Judge was Beverly Briley (first elected in 1950). An attorney, Briley has received widespread recognition, having been elected president of the National Association of County Officials. But Briley is considered somewhat different from West in his political philosophy—less "liberal" and less oriented toward the central city. He is considered something of a financial conservative and a champion less of urban than of suburban causes. Two of his major achievements as County Judge, for example, consisted of instituting a new system of budget control and gaining for Davidson County an "AA" bond rating. In addition, Briley readily acknowledges his eagerness to defend the suburbanite. He has publicly deplored the "open season" declared on the suburbanite by such "sophisticated magazines" as the *New Yorker, Harpers,* and *Atlantic* which, he offers, "outdo each other in coining names for this class of Americans."[6]

NASHVILLE'S METROPOLITAN PROBLEMS

Although some of Nashville's metropolitan problems are unique, many of them are similar to those of other medium-sized

6. Beverly Briley, "Keynote Address Before the Urban County Congress, The National Association of County Officials," New York, March 15, 1959, p. 4.

metropolitan areas. The central city, for example, has suffered the usual financial disadvantages; and financial resources are unequally distributed. Also, there was no areawide instrumentality to handle areawide problems until 1962. The existence, moreover, of fifteen units of government dispersed and rendered more difficult popular control over local government. Finally, the area's suburbs, like other suburbs in the early stages of metropolitan growth, were and largely remain without the usual municipal services such as fire and police protection, garbage collection, and in some cases water supply. In most Nashville suburbs fire and police protection, and garbage collection were provided, and still are, on a private subscription basis.

On the other hand, the Nashville area presents some unique features. Perhaps one of the most significant of these stems from the nature of the area's subsoil. Much of it is either rocky or solid rock, making septic tanks unsatisfactory in some places and the installation of sewers unusually expensive. As will be seen, the absence of sewers in the suburban areas has long been one of Nashville's most serious service problems.

Although not entirely unique, the Nashville area has relatively few governmental units compared with some metropolitan areas. Before consolidation the area contained six incorporated communities[7] in addition to the City of Nashville, seven special districts,[8] and one county, for a total of 15 governmental units to serve 399,743 people. In contrast, the Tulsa area in 1962 contained 124 units for 418,974 people, and Salt Lake City had 30 units for 383,035 people. On the other hand, Richmond's metropolitan area contained only 5 governmental units to serve 408,494 people.[9]

7. They were Belle Meade, Oak Hill, Forest Hills, Berry Hill, Goodlettsville, and Dupontonia (now Lakewood). The first three were incorporated primarily to shield exclusive residential domains through zoning regulations. Lakewood and Goodlettsville were incorporated after the 1958 Metro vote.

8. They included six utility districts and the Nashville Housing Authority. The latter is considered a special district by the U. S. Bureau of the Census.

9. Population figures are from the 1960 *Census of Population*. Governmental unit figures are from the 1962 *Census of Governments*.

IMPLICATIONS OF THE SETTING

Before consolidation the Nashville area was dominated by a county-based politician, Beverly Briley, and a city-based politician, Ben West; but as we have seen the two did not enjoy equal power. West commanded more administrative authority than did his counterpart; more important, he presided over a well-run political organization based on city employees. Briley had no comparable organization in the county, although he did have several supporters among county officials. Briley also had the backing of the larger of the two metropolitan newspapers, the morning Nashville *Tennessean.* The Nashville *Banner,* on the other hand, was a West supporter and had been since West's first campaign for mayor in 1951.

Nashville's political situation was thus characterized by an uneven division of power, but there existed certain conditions that raised the possibility of redressing, even inverting, the balance. Paramount among these was the lack of sewers and other municipal services in the urbanized fringe outside the City of Nashville. Potentially significant also was the existence of an entrenched city political machine, a phenomenon which many citizens found most offensive.

This author is not contending, let it be noted, that Briley perceived the potential utility of these conditions when the Metro idea first appeared in Nashville and that he saw Metro as a device for exploiting them. Our point is simply that such potentially important conditions did exist, and that in the end Beverly Briley was elected mayor of the new metropolitan government. On November 6, 1962, he decisively defeated Clifford Allen, former state senator and at the time of the election Davidson County Tax Assessor. Ben West, who had supported the 1958 Metro charter but strongly opposed the 1962 charter, did not choose to make the race.

4

PROPOSITIONS ABOUT OPPOSITION
AND SUPPORT FOR
METROPOLITAN INTEGRATION

As already noted, governmental reorganization attempts in metropolitan areas have met with few concrete successes, despite widespread interest and sometimes strenuous efforts. Most conspicuous of the recent defeats were the Greater St. Louis City–County District and the Cuyahoga County (Cleveland) home rule charter. Other major defeats since 1950 include consolidation proposals in Nashville–Davidson County in 1958, Albuquerque–Bernalillo County, Knoxville–Knox County, Memphis–Shelby County, Macon–Bibb County, and Richmond–Henrico County. In Nashville, Macon, and Richmond the referenda were voted down because of negative votes outside the city. In Knoxville, Albuquerque, and Memphis, however, both central city and fringe areas voted against the proposed consolidation.[1]

Writing before the Nashville consolidation occurred, Charles R. Adrian reported that in all at least fifteen attempts have been made to consolidate a city and a county in the twentieth century, with only the 1947 combination of Baton Rouge and East Baton Rouge Parish succeeding.[2]

1. Advisory Commission on Intergovernmental Relations, *Factors Affecting Voter Reactions to Governmental Reorganization in Metropolitan Areas* (Washington, D. C., 1962).

2. Adrian, *Governing Urban America* (New York: McGraw Hill, 1961), p. 284. He failed to include the 1952 consolidation of Phoebus, Hampton, and Elizabeth City County, Virginia.

Most of the reorganization proposals that the voters have approved in recent years, moreover, involved little structural change. Three metropolitan counties in the state of New York, for example, gained voter acceptance for proposals dealing only with the reorganization of their county governments. These were Erie County (Buffalo), Onondaga County (Syracuse), and Oneida County (Utica). Other proposals that have successfully met the test of popular referendum include a Seattle Special Purpose District, a Denver Metropolitan Capitol Improvement District,[3] an Atlanta–Fulton County "Plan of Improvement,"[4] and the Miami –Dade County plan.

The past history of such efforts, then, provides little basis for optimism about the prospects for major governmental reorganization in metropolitan areas. Many of the most qualified students have concluded (often reluctantly) that this is the case. Victor Jones has said, for example,

> the one clear lesson we all should have learned by now from the many attempts in this country and abroad to establish metropolitan governments in that units of local government are tough organizations with many political and legal protections against annihilation or absorption by another government.[5]

In a similar vein, Adrian has said that consolidation is not likely to bear much fruit in the future.[6] And as long ago as 1941 John A. Rush concluded that attempts to consolidate are bound to fail when a vote is required.[7]

---

3. Adopted, September 1961; declared unconstitutional, February 13, 1962.

4. The Atlanta proposal (1950) included a large annexation. The proposal in that city required a majority in both Atlanta and the area to be annexed. This was achieved.

5. "Local Government Organization in Metropolitan Areas," in *"The Future of Cities and Urban Redevelopment,* ed. Coleman Woodbury (Chicago: University of Chicago Press, 1953), p. 587.

6. Adrian, *op. cit.,* p. 284.

7. *The City-County Consolidated* (Los Angeles: By the Author, 1941), p. 365.

VOTER OPPOSITION AND SUPPORT:
SOME HYPOTHESES

Dissatisfaction with Public Services under a Fragmented Structure: The Satisfaction with Services Variable. "It is frequently assumed that the impetus for governmental change in metropolitan areas is generated by widespread dissatisfaction with services."[8] One of the cardinal tenets of the metropolitan reform movement is that if governmental structure is "fragmented" and "irrational" the citizen will respond through general dissatisfaction and criticism.[9] Is there such a ground swell of popular dissatisfaction? Recent research would seem to indicate that there is not.

In Flint, Michigan, opinion surveys uncovered little serious dissatisfaction. More than 90 per cent of those interviewed in the central city were satisfied with most of their services. Education, streets and roads, and street lighting pleased somewhat fewer people, but four people out of every five interviewed expressed satisfaction. There was, however, a greater proportion of dissatisfied citizens on the fringes, particularly with regard to sewage disposal (33 per cent dissatisfied), streets and roads (37 per cent dissatisfied), and street lighting (49 per cent dissatisfied). Nevertheless, no service was felt to be unsatisfactory by as many as half of the fringe residents.[10]

Bollens found in his Dayton study that in the area as a whole no governmental service evoked dissatisfaction from as much as half the population. Many people were not displeased with any

8. Henry J. Schmandt *et al., Metropolitan Reform in St. Louis: A Case Study* (New York: Holt, Rinehart and Winston, 1961), p. 63.
9. Scott Greer, "Dilemmas of Action Research on the Metropolitan Problem," in *Community Political Systems,* ed. Morris Janowitz (Glencoe, Illinois: The Free Press, 1961), p. 197.
10. Amos H. Hawley and Basil G. Zimmer, "Resistance to Unification in a Metropolitan Community," in *Community Political Systems,* ed. Morris Janowitz (Glencoe, Illinois: The Free Press, 1961), pp. 164–167.

service.[11] In St. Louis a large proportion indicated some dissatisfaction (approximately 80 per cent had some suggestions for
changes or improvements), but there was very little consensus as
to the changes desired and there was no significant criticism of
most major services of government. Thus fewer than 10 per cent
indicated they desired improvements in any of these services:
police protection, fire protection, water supply, garbage, trash
and sewage disposal, or pollution control. Schools, the subject
of continual agitation, were identified as "problem areas" by
fewer than 5 per cent of the subjects in the area. A very few indicated a desire for lower taxes.[12] Only recreation, traffic, and
transportation drew responses of dissatisfaction from more than
17 per cent of those interviewed. No strong criticism was expressed against any of the governments. Only one unit—the
metropolitan sewer district—was considered to be performing
poorly by as many as 10 per cent of the respondents.[13]

After the failure in 1959 of the proposed Greater St. Louis
Metropolitan District, one local political leader observed that
reorganization would only be possible "when an obviously bad
breakdown in existing local government occurs or when there
is a manifest economic interest at stake for the voters."[14] As
shown above there was "no general feeling of urgency" in St.
Louis despite rather heavy expressions of dislike for the status
quo (60 per cent in the city and 57 per cent in the county).

One hypothesis implied by these findings and conclusions is
that voters who are dissatisfied with services are more likely to
support reorganization than voters who are satisfied. This is
perhaps the most common hypothesis and is the one that is
tested here.

*Anticipation of Higher Taxes With Reorganization: The Cost
Variable.* It seems likely that voters will oppose metropolitan

11. John C. Bollens *et al., Metropolitan Challenge* (Dayton, Ohio:
Metropolitan Community Studies Incorporated, 1959), p. 241.
12. Scott Greer, *op. cit.,* p. 197, 198.
13. Schmandt *et al., op. cit.,* p. 63.
14. *Ibid.,* p. 71.

reorganization when they feel it will bring higher taxes. The fact that the opposition to reorganization often raises the spectre of higher taxes adds to the plausibility of this explanation.

Yet it is conceivable that voters will be persuaded that reorganization will save them money, or at least enable them to get more for their tax dollar by ending duplication and waste. This argument is frequently stressed by the proponents of integration. In Nashville, as we shall see below, these divergent views concerning the effect of metropolitan integration on taxes clashed openly.

It is also quite possible that voters will be willing to accept higher taxes if the taxes bring better services. Research in Flint found that fringe occupants said they were "willing to accept higher taxes in order to secure better services."[15] A majority of all categories of respondents, except the "nonworking," indicated receptivity to higher taxes; and fringe residents were more favorably disposed than were central city residents. "It hardly seems likely," the authors conclude, "that governmental unification is resisted on the basis of increased costs to individual taxpayers which might follow the event."[16]

Another possibility is that the voter feels he is getting his tax money's worth under the existing "fragmented" structure. Respondents in Dayton were asked whether local taxes were too high, too low, or about right in view of what they were getting from their local government. Two thirds felt that taxes were "about right." Three per cent felt they were "too low."

When a voter expresses such a feeling, however, it may be that the more salient consideration is not that he is getting his money's worth "now" but that he *does not want an increase*. In other words, he may be saying simply that "everything is O.K. as is; let's not change." This may be another way of expressing fear or dislike for higher taxes if the status quo is upset.

What kind of light do the Nashville data shed on the relation-

15. Hawley and Zimmer, *op. cit.,* p. 173.
16. *Ibid.,* pp. 173, 174.

ship between voter anticipation of higher taxes with reorganization and opposition to reorganization? Perhaps the most common proposition in the literature is that where there is such voter anticipation there will be opposition, although other propositions are plausible. The hypothesis tested below is the more common one—that those voters who anticipate higher taxes with reorganization are more likely to oppose it than those who do not anticipate higher taxes. This hypothesis assumes that the majority of voters who anticipate higher taxes with reorganization find the prospect of more taxes very distasteful.

Suburban and Rural Suspicion of the City and Its Government: The Geographic Variable.   Suburbanites and those living still farther out are often suspicious of the central city government and its motives. They sometimes view proposals for metropolitan integration in terms of the city reaching out to swallow them up. Of course large numbers of suburbanites once lived in the city and believe that living there again would be unbearable. One must also keep in mind that to many suburbanites "atomized" or "fragmented" governmental structure is not at all undesirable. On the contrary, fifty-three fire departments are often viewed as highly desirable in terms of the "grass roots" philosophy and keeping government "close to the people." Robert C. Wood has suggested that suburban communities, which are regarded by reformers as "satellite cities" and impediments to rational, area-wide government, are viewed by suburbanites themselves as ideal grass-roots communities and as heirs apparent to the great American small town.[17]

The survey research undertaken in this area supports the proposition that fringe distaste for the central city is fairly widespread, thus providing at least a foundation for antireorganization sentiment. In Flint, for example, people viewed city government less favorably than township government.[18] In Dayton a majority

17. *Suburbia: Its People and Their Politics* (Boston: Houghton Mifflin, 1959).
18. Hawley and Zimmer, *op. cit.*, pp. 175, 176.

of surburban city residents expressed a preference for their own community having a separate government.[19]

The hypothesis implied here is that where there is suspicion there will be resistance. The hypothesis tested below, therefore, is that outside voters suspicious of the central city are more likely to oppose reorganization that those who are not suspicious. This hypothesis uses the word "suspicious" only to convey the attitude widely attributed in the literature to fringe residents and is based on the widespread notion that "outside" voters sometimes view a proposed governmental reorganization as the city reaching out to get them. Thus they oppose such reorganization.[20]

"Ignorance" and Unfamiliarity with Local Government Generally and Metropolitan Issues in Particular: The Knowledge Variable. In the literature there is strong documentation for the conclusion that many voters are ignorant about government. Large numbers cannot name their officials, nor are they familiar with important public issues. In Flint, for example, two fifths of the fringe residents were unable to name the occupant of a single official position, and only about one third could name more than two.[21] The authors of the Flint study were brought to the conclusion, at least tentatively, that resistance to governmental unification rests largely upon ignorance of government and what to expect from it. Further support for this conclusion was adduced by the fact that proannexation sentiment was concentrated among the highly educated respondents.[22]

What light do the Nashville data shed on the relationship between voter ignorance and resistance to metropolitan reorgani-

19. Bollens *et. al., op. cit.,* p. 259.
20. In Nashville (1962), however, there was considerable reason to expect the opposite because the city had recently annexed a very sizeable chunk of county territory, thus raising the possibility that anticity (antiannexation) sentiment would be proreorganization sentiment. In other words, the possibility existed that suspicion of the city, by reason of the recent annexation, might not lead to opposition to consolidation, but to support for it as preferable to further annexations.
21. Hawley and Zimmer, *op. cit.,* pp. 176, 178.
22. *Ibid.,* p. 182.

zation? The proposition implied from the research cited above is that where there is voter ignorance there will be resistance. The hypothesis tested below is that less well-informed voters are more likely to oppose reorganization than better-informed voters. The reader is admonished that this hypothesis is not intended to relate directly to the "class" variable, whether class is measured by income or education. The focus is on voter ignorance and knowledge.

In summary, these hypotheses about voters may be listed: voters who are dissatisfied with services are more likely to support reorganization than those who are satisfied; voters who anticipate higher taxes with reorganization are more likely to oppose reorganization than those who do not anticipate higher taxes; voters outside the central city who are "suspicious" of the city are more likely to oppose reorganization than those who are not "suspicious"; voters who are less knowledgeable are more likely to oppose reorganization than those who are more knowledgeable.

INTEREST GROUP OPPOSITION AND SUPPORT

In its study of eighteen reorganization attempts since 1950, the Advisory Commission on Intergovernmental Relations listed, among others, the following community elements as "predominantly favoring" reorganization: metropolitan newspapers, Leagues of Women Voters, central city chambers of commerce, central city officials, academic spokesmen, and central city commercial and real estate interests.[23] Other studies have been consistent with the Advisory Commission's findings. Thus Victor Jones also found that downtown merchants and chambers of commerce tend to be proreorganization,[24] and Edward Sofen found Miami's downtown merchants taking a similar stand.[25]

23. Advisory Commission on Intergrovernmental Relations, *op. cit.,* pp. 5, 6.
24. *Metropolitan Government* (Chicago: University of Chicago Press, 1942), pp. 254–259.
25. *A Report on Politics in Greater Miami* (Cambridge: Joint Center for Urban Studies of MIT and Harvard University, 1961), Chap. 5, p. 23.

The survey of eighteen cities by the Advisory Commission on Intergovernmental Relations found that the following groups, among others, commonly opposed reorganization: farmers and rural homeowners, county government employees, and employees of fringe local governments.

This study proposes to treat these findings as hypotheses for further examination. The hypotheses to be examined in light of the Nashville experience are that groups in the first list above tend to support governmental reorganization in metropolitan areas and that groups in the second list tend to oppose it.

5

THE FORMATIVE YEARS: 1951–1958

RECENT historical considerations bear heavily on the 1962 referendum. It is therefore necessary to understand something of the background of that referendum, particularly the decade preceding it, for it was during these years that several important issues were born and nurtured.[1]

As already noted, Nashville's municipal government was reorganized in 1947. In that same year a group of local government officials began to meet informally to discuss metropolitan problems. The local political reporters of the two metropolitan newspapers, the *Tennessean* and the *Banner*, also attended these meetings.[2]

In 1951 Nashville elected a new mayor, Ben West, who was opposed by the *Tennessean* and supported by the *Banner*. A year earlier Beverly Briley had been elected to the county judgeship, also for the first time.

The new County Judge had advocated in his campaign a thorough study of Davidson County government, and shortly thereafter the Tennessee Taypayers' Association undertook such a study. Among the many recommendations of the resulting report was the following: "The governmental needs of a metropolitan community such as Davidson County could be most efficiently

1. Some of the material in this chapter and the next is told elsewhere. It is repeated here solely to provide a complete description of the metropolitan integration process in Nashville.

2. Daniel J. Elazar, *A Case Study of Failure In Attempted Metropolitan Integration: Nashville and Davidson County, Tennessee* (Chicago: National Opinion Research Center of the University of Chicago, 1961), p. 30.

and economically served by one completely consolidated unit of local government."[3] Because of constitutional obstacles, however, it was felt that little could then be accomplished in the way of consolidation.

That same year the Davidson County delegation to the Tennessee legislature secured the passage of a private act creating a "Community Services Commission for Davidson County and the City of Nashville." The city and the county supplied funds jointly, and the task set for the Community Services Commission was to "survey the governmental needs of metropolitan Nashville and Davidson County and to suggest ways of supplying these needs."[4] The report of this Commission, published in 1952, became a milestone in the Nashville story and it is therefore necessary to consider it at some length.[5]

The preamble to the private act creating the Commission set forth the basic problem:

> it is hereby found and declared that the great concentration of people and their homes, institutions and enterprises occupying the central portion of Davidson County constitute substantially one community and have a common need for those services and facilities customarily supplied by a local government formed for such purpose; that less than two thirds of the population comprising this area are served by such a local government. . . .[6]

A Future For Nashville, as the resulting report was called, concentrated on the suburban area immediately outside the City of

3. Tennessee Taxpayers' Association, *Report on a Detailed Survey of the Financial Condition of Davidson County, Tennessee, With Recommendations*, Nashville, October, 1951, Section IV, p. iv.

4. Community Services Commission for Davidson County and the City of Nashville, *A Future for Nashville: Summary of Findings and Recommendations* (Nashville, 1952), p. 1.

5. The staff of the Community Services Commission was directed by two political scientists — Lee S. Greene of the University of Tennessee and (Assistant Director) Daniel R. Grant of Vanderbilt University. Its chairman was a Nashville attorney, Edwin F. Hunt, who subsequently became an outstanding figure among the proponents of consolidation and one that is met frequently in the Nashville story.

6. Community Services Commission for Davidson County and the City of Nashville, *op. cit.*, p. 1.

Nashville, an area then comprising about sixty-nine square miles and ninety thousand people. A major theme of the report was that the central city ought to furnish the suburban area's urban services and that an immediate annexation program ought to be undertaken to make this possible. The report also stated that Nashville could not hope to grow, or even hold its own, while obsolete city limits excluded more than ninety thousand urban dwellers.[7]

In 1952, however, the annexation of county territory in Tennessee could only be accomplished by private act of the legislature or by petition and affirmative vote by those outside the central city. The method recommended by the Community Services Commission was that the Davidson County legislative delegation (by private act) provide for an advisory referendum to determine the wishes of the voters concerning annexation. Upon the affirmative vote of a majority of those in the entire urbanized area, consisting of the suburban area and the City of Nashville taken together, the delegation should then proceed to extend the city limits by private act of the General Assembly.[8] The objective behind this single-majority strategy, of course, was to overcome an anticipated negative vote in the suburbs with a heavily proannexation vote in the old city.

The second major recommendation of the Community Services Commission was that the county be given exclusive authority to provide certain areawide services (the obverse of urban services by the municipality). Specifically, the Commission recommended making the county exclusively responsible for public health services, hospital care for indigents, public schools, and public welfare.

The Commission also recommended that Davidson County be redistricted by the General Assembly in order to give equitable representation in the Quarterly Court to urban residents. Finally, it commented favorably upon city-county consolidation but noted

7. *Ibid.,* p. 15.
8. *Ibid.*

that because of constitutional obstacles it was not then a feasible course of action.

The net result of the Community Services Commission's efforts was to transfer the city health department and the city juvenile court to Davidson County. The annexation proposal—the heart of the study—was not acted upon by the legislature.

Then on June 4, 1953, the Tennessee Constitution was amended to permit the consolidation of any or all functions of cities and counties upon the affirmative vote of a majority of those voting within the municipality and those voting in the county outside. The amendment was not self-executing, however; actual consolidation would require enabling legislation from the General Assembly. It nevertheless provided an important breakthrough for advocates of city-county consolidation by removing certain legal obstacles[9] which had forced both the Tennessee Taxpayers' Association and the Community Services Commission to treat city-county consolidation as an unfeasible approach to the Nashville area's problems.

Another important link in the Nashville story was supplied two years later when the Tennessee legislature enacted a statute that permitted municipalities *to annex by ordinance alone*, with court review of the reasonableness of the annexation available.[10] Before 1955, Tennessee municipalities had been unable to annex except by means of a private act of the legislature or by petition from those outside.[11]

9. One of the stickiest problems involved the necessity of having (in effect) two different tax rates in the county when the Tennessee Constitution required an equal and uniform tax rate for all property. Two tax rates were necessary because of the vast differences between the rural and urban sections of the county. Another impediment involved the abridgement of the terms of the "constitutional officers," i.e., those established by constitutional provision. If the legislature had authorized such an abridgement, this would have pitted the Constitution against the statute, with doubtful consequences for consolidation.

10. Later this statute was amended to require that the annexing municipality have a definite plan for extending services to the annexed area.

11. Actually a 1953 constitutional amendment had banned the former method. So between 1953 and 1955 petition was the only available method of annexation in Tennessee.

DEVELOPING THE STRATEGY FOR METROPOLITAN GOVERNMENT

By this time it had become clear to local reformers that the report of the Community Services Commission, however well considered, would not lead to any substantial solution to the problems of metropolitan Nashville. But reform-minded people in the area were still concerned about such problems. The Nashville Chamber of Commerce, for example, had already established a so-called Greater Nashville Committee, composed of Chamber members, to discuss fresh approaches to the area's metropolitan problems. The Greater Nashville Committee then decided to make a formal study of the subject and to seek the aid of the City and County Planning Commissions in doing so. As it happened, many of the planners were also members of the Chamber; there thus emerged a rather classic overlapping of public and private bodies in the resulting study group. Also included were the mayor and the county judge, by virtue of their membership on the planning commissions.

On June 21, 1955, the County Judge made a speech before the Rotary Club in which he urged the adoption of a single government for Nashville and Davidson County. This was the first public statement concerning "Metro" to be made by a local political leader.

Meanwhile the city and county planners were entering the picture in yet another capacity. Two years earlier, in 1953, an "Advance Planning and Research Division" had been established (by private act amendment to the city charter) to undertake long-range research and planning projects.[12] In the summer of 1955 the Planning Commissions authorized the Advance Planning Division to initiate a series of long-range studies. Among the studies authorized were ones relating to building sewers in the surburban area and to governmental structure. A firm of engineers was hired to make the sewer study. To help with the study

12. The Advance Planning and Research Division was provided with a $50,000 revolving fund to allay expenses. Mr. Irving Hand, an MIT graduate, was made Director.

of governmental structure, Daniel R. Grant, Vanderbilt University political scientist, was hired. There followed a series of discussions that may well rank among the most crucial ever held in Nashville and Davidson County.

The chief participants in these important discussions were Irving Hand, Director of the Advance Planning Division; Charles W. Hawkins, Executive Director of the two Planning Commissions; Robert Horton, Research Director for the Advance Planning Division; and Professor Grant, serving as consultant.

While the governmental structure study was under way, the engineers brought in tentative recommendations for a special sewer district—a course of action not uncommon for utilities consultants concerned with only one segment of a metropolitan area's problems. Hand, Hawkins, Grant, and Horton, however, felt that such an approach was not satisfactory from several standpoints. They considered special districts to be poorly designed for purposes of democratic control and also regarded them as an aggravation of the basic problem of too many governmental units in the metropolitan area. It was felt in addition that a sewer district would constitute a piecemeal approach which might, by solving the number-one problem, delay indefinitely community pressure sufficient to bring about a solution to such additional problems as fire and police protection, parks, and schools. The tactic here was to avoid small improvements that might block a more thoroughgoing change.

In any event, the skull sessions held by Hawkins, Hand, Horton, and Grant produced the following grand strategy (perhaps "stratagem" is a more appropriate term): *annexation in the short run and city-county consolidation in the long run.* This was the basic formula, and it was designed to win over the political titans of the metropolitan area—Mayor West and Judge Briley. The sticking point was that Mayor West preferred annexation and the Judge consolidation.

The strategists took the preferences of each man into account, and they considered it quite possible that the Mayor, on the one hand, would doubt that consolidation could be achieved, and the Judge, on the other, would doubt the likelihood of achieving any substantial annexation. They thus hoped that each man might conclude that *his* preference was the attainable one. There were ample grounds for both conclusions, and the result would be to make the "package proposal" acceptable to each.

With this Machiavellian strategy, the group presented a draft of the two-pronged "Plan of Metropolitan Government" to the city and county planning commissions (including Mayor West and Judge Briley) for their consideration. This undertaking nearly killed their strategy before it could be applied, for Mayor West, who preferred annexation and was perhaps worried about his areawide support, was anything but enthusiastic. After many weeks of discussion, persuasion, and revision, however, the two commissions came to unanimous agreement on publication and release of the plan for public consideration. Immediate annexation was still recommended, but far greater emphasis was given to a comprehensive plan for city-county consolidation. The end product was, in all major respects, the consolidation plan that six years later was to be adopted in the Nashville metropolitan area.

On October 30, 1956, the plan was released and a copy of it printed in the local newspapers. Both the *Banner* and the *Tennessean* ran four-page inserts entitled a "Plan of Metropolitan Government for Nashville and Davidson County." The insert described in some detail the "metropolitan problem," including specific references to the "absence of a sanitary sewer system" and poor fire and police protection outside the City of Nashville. Besides such service deficiencies, reference was also made to the fact that there was no existing government able to cope with areawide problems. A subheading declared that "the existence of separate city and county governments is not only wasteful to the extent that there is duplication of government, but it also tends to divide the loyalties of community leadership and the authority of local government at times when unity is urgently needed."

Another section evaluated alternatives. Annexation was described as meritorious but difficult to achieve—and no solution in any case to conflict and duplication between city and county. Also considered were functional consolidation, special utility districts, federation, expansion of county functions, and city-county separation. All were found wanting, largely because they were regarded as less complete solutions than consolidation.

The largest portion of the insert was devoted to the actual proposal, with questions and answers about its provisions. Briefly, its major features were as follows:

The metropolitan government would exercise its jurisdiction within two service districts. A "general services district" would provide all "those general services which are required on an areawide basis" and encompass the area of the entire county. An "urban services district," comprising the City of Nashville, would provide additional urban services normally required in an urban area. There would be two different tax levies corresponding to the services rendered; there would be a single chief executive with the administrative authority commonly possessed by a strong mayor; and there would be a single legislative body for the entire area. Finally a "Plan of Action" was presented. It called for the creation of a broadly based citizens' organization to disseminate information on the plan; and it proposed a definite schedule of action:

Early 1957: Passage of an enabling act by the Tennessee General Assembly authorizing the creation of single metropolitan governments. (Such an act would apply the 1953 constitutional amendment.)

May, 1957: Creation of a metropolitan government charter commission for Nashville and Davidson County, as authorized by the enabling act.

February 1, 1958: Completion of a draft for consolidation by the charter commission.

May, 1958: Referendum on adoption of charter.

August, 1958: Election to choose officers for the new metropolitan government.

September 1, 1958: Date for the metropolitan government to go into effect.

This was a bold plan indeed. The first step was to secure the necessary enabling act. To accomplish this the planning commissions turned to attorney Edwin F. Hunt (mentioned earlier as chairman of the Community Services Commission) for assistance in drafting the bill. But to get the desired action by the General Assembly it was first necessary to line up the Davidson County delegation behind the proposal. To this end a series of public hearings was held, and both opponents and proponents were invited to air their views. With the exception of some "machine" politicians in the city, little opposition appeared at these hearings. The Davidson County delegation thus agreed to support the proposed enabling act.

Once the local legislative delegation was won over, the rest of the legislature became the objective. Overtures were first made to the delegations from the other three metropolitan counties in Tennessee. After a series of meetings between the Davidson County delegation and the delegations from the other metropolitan counties, and with the persuasive efforts of County Judge Briley, their support was secured. Shelby County (Memphis) was hesitant at first but was won over by promises of support for some of its measures and, apparently, by the desire of its delegation to maintain a "progressive" reputation.

Overtures were next made to the state's rural legislators, who formed the vast majority of the Assembly. Once again Judge Briley (then President of the Tennessee Association of County Officials) worked hard, and once again promises of support were traded. After an agreement that, among other things, state sales tax distributions would be made only to the "urban services district" of any consolidation and not to the whole consolidated county, the rural legislators were placated.[13]

13. This description of how support was secured from the Davidson County delegation, and from the rest of the General Assembly, comes from Daniel J. Elazar, *op. cit.,* pp. 23–25. Elazar interviewed several legislators.

In February 1957 the measure[14] passed both houses with but one negative vote in each chamber. It was signed by the governor in March.

The new consolidation law provided for consolidations only in those counties having a population of 200,000 or more. Consolidations were to be accomplished through a new political entity, a third form of government, called a "metropolitan government," which was to do the job previously done by the county and the city and to have all the powers of each. The initial step in any proposed consolidation was to be the creation of a "charter commission." Under the enabling act such a charter commission could only be created by similar resolutions of the county governing body and the city governing body.[15]

The 1957 consolidation law also contained rather detailed provisions as to how the charter commission was to function and what provisions the resulting charter should contain. Among the provisions, for example, was that there be two taxing districts, one for general services and one for urban services.

THE 1958 CHARTER COMMISSION AND ITS WORK

Directly upon the heels of the consolidation act's passage, the county quarterly court and the city council moved to form the required charter commission. Both legislative bodies officially supported the creation of such a body,[16] although loud protests were heard in the quarterly court from Ewing Clouse, magistrate from the tiny city of Berry Hill and inveterate champion of suburban incorporations. The members selected by the county judge (and approved by the quarterly court) included a state senator who had led the fight for enabling legislation in the upper cham-

14. See *Tennessee Code Annotated,* Chapter 37, Sections 6-3701 through 6-3723.

15. Creation by popular initiative was also considered but discarded when the Nashville and Davidson County governing bodies promised to authorize a charter commission. In 1961 this provision was amended to provide that a charter commission might also be created in the manner prescribed by private act.

16. The Quarterly Court voted 30–18; the City Council had but two negative votes.

ber, a leading industrialist, a local businessman, a Negro community leader, and an attorney who had been a labor-endorsed state representative. The mayor's choices (approved by the city council) included a prominent woman attorney, an elementary school principal from a lower-income neighborhood, a labor leader, a Negro city councilman, and two prominent attorneys.

In the selection of the members of the commission much attention was given to the question of representativeness. All but one of the commission members felt when asked that they had been chosen in part for representative purpose.[17] The strategy here was to turn out a proposal with the support of, and indeed written by, leading figures from several of the major elements in the community—higher-income, teachers, Negro, labor, business. Even if one of these groups latter refused to endorse the proposal, the pro-Metro forces could at least point out that a leading figure in the group supported it.

The charter commission proceeded to get to work with staff assistance from the Planning Commissions' Advance Planning Division. An attorney, E. C. Yokely, was employed as executive secretary. Toward the end of the commission's work, Edwin F. Hunt was employed as legal consultant.

All meetings of the Commission were open to the public, and eleven sessions were expressly devoted to hearing the view of interested individuals or groups. Except for the press, however, they were poorly attended.

It was not surprising that the question of Negro support for consolidation entered prominently into the deliberations of the charter commission. Having gained two seats on the existing city council and with excellent prospects for more, the Negroes were concerned about their representation.[18] From one point of view, of course, consolidation could be considered a bald contrivance for

17. David Grubbs, "City-County Consolidation Attempts in Nashville and Knoxville, Tennessee" (unpublished Ph.D. dissertation, Department of Political Science, University of Pennsylvania, 1961), p. 218.
18. See above Chapter Three for the percentage of nonwhites in the Nashville area.

diluting the growing Negro vote in the old city. Many Negroes—
and whites as well—so considered it. It must be borne in mind
that although Negro registration and voting have not been ob-
structed in Nashville, Negroes have in the past suffered numerous
gerrymanders.[19]

In any event, the charter commission drew up the metropolitan
councilmanic districts so that at least two seats on the new council
would be held by Negroes. In all, fifteen councilmen were to be
elected from roughly equal districts, and six were to be chosen at
large. This total (twenty-one) was about one third of the number
of representatives on the existing city and county legislative
bodies.

The new metropolitan government was to be divided into the
two taxing districts proposed in 1956 by the planning commission.[20] Areas outside the urban services district could be "annexed" to the urban services district by simple ordinance. In
addition, the four incorporated communities in the county,
excluding Nashville, were to retain their present independent
status until (or unless) they decided to merge with the consolidated government.

19. Daniel J. Elazar, *op. cit.*, pp. 64–66.
20. The allocation of services to the two service districts took the following form:

Urban Services District	General Services District	
police (class I)	general administration	police
fire protection (class III)	fire protection	courts
water	assessment	jails
sewers, sanitary	hospitals	health
sewers, storm	streets and roads	welfare
street lighting	parks and recreation	traffic
refuse collection and disposal	auditorium	schools
wine and whiskey supervision	fair grounds	library
taxicab regulation	public housing	airport
	urban redevelopment	zoning
	electricity	transit
	building code	planning
	plumbing code	
	electrical code	
	housing code	

THE 1958 CAMPAIGN

Even before the 1958 charter commission had completed its task, support was growing in the community. The Nashville Chamber of Commerce, of course, was one of Metro's leading supporters and had already been active for some time; in fact, the Chamber's Board of Governors formally endorsed the plan within a month of its publication. The League of Women Voters also immediately endorsed the Metro idea,[21] as did the Nashville Trades and Labor Council. The latter called upon the area's union members to support it. The Tennessee Taxpayer's Association (a spokesman for business and commercial interests), and the Tennessee Municipal League also endorsed consolidation.

Both Nashville newspapers supported Metro, as did various civic leaders, professors, the Mayor, County Judge, and about one half of the city councilmen and county magistrates.[22] Some observers felt, however, that the citizenry did not uniformly accept as genuine the endorsements of politicians. Charges and counter-charges, carried by word of mouth, reportedly claimed that many politicians publicly supported Metro because they saw this as the popular thing to do but privately opposed it because they feared the loss of their jobs with consolidation.[23]

It is noteworthy also that the county judge's personal support slackened considerably before the referendum. His explanation was that he became involved, in the months preceding the vote, in a campaign for re-election. Even after the April 10, 1958, Democratic primary resulted in his renomination, however, he never resumed his previous level of activity. Perhaps he feared that the opponents of Metro would enter a candidate against him in the August general election. Perhaps he lost some of his

21. The day before the vote that League of Women Voters organized two hundred phone callers in behalf of Metro.
22. Bertil Hanson, *A Report on Politics in Nashville* (Cambridge: Joint Center for Urban Studies of MIT and Harvard University, 1960), Chapter 6, p. 8.
23. Interview, Robert Horton, Director of Research Nashville–Davidson County Planning Commission, November 11, 1962.

enthusiasm for the campaign through fear that West was the more likely choice for metropolitan mayor.

It was further charged that the Judge more than tapered off— that he actually opposed consolidation "under the table" when it appeared that it might win, and he might lose. This charge was made by a former newspaper reporter and also by a prominent city councilman, both supporters of Clifford Allen's 1962 campaign against Briley for metropolitan mayor. Others have suggested that Briley did not have a "county machine" (such as West allegedly had in the city) and thus was unable to deliver the county vote.

In addition to the above individuals and groups, supporters of Metro set up a special citizen's committee to direct their campaign. Again initial impetus came from the Chamber of Commerce, although it in turn was prodded by the planners.[24] The original citizens' committee consisted of nineteen members including Chamber people, the mayor, the county judge, officers of the League of Women Voters, the President of the Nashville Trades and Labor Council, officers of the local PTA, the Director of Research of the State Planning Commission, the President of the Junior Chamber of Commerce, a Negro community leader, a suburban magistrate, a physician, and an attorney.

No important opposition appeared at this stage, and perhaps partly for this reason the citizen's committee never really got off the ground. It did sponsor a speakers' bureau, distribute literature, and print copies of the proposed charter, but its general record reveals few bright spots.[25] The stage was set for failure by the fact, for example, that the committee undertook in its first few meetings to declare its unwillingness to support Metro without first thoroughly examining the proposal. According to the committee's secretary, nearly ten months were spent "arguing whether a Citizens' Committee for Metro should actively campaign for Metro or should limit itself to presenting both sides of the ques-

24. Daniel J. Elazar, *op. cit.*, p. 28.
25. *Ibid.*

tion."[26] This was indeed an inauspicious beginning for an organization designed not to debate Metro but to secure its passage.[27]

In any event, the committee distributed copies of the proposed charter and a rather long descriptive brochure and sponsored radio and television talks. The primary objective, it was felt, was to "explain" the charter and the problems occasioning its birth. Obviously this type of campaign reaches the kind of people who read the papers, watch rather "dull" television talks, attend meetings, and are able to understand such complex matters as are contained in a consolidation charter. It probably does not reach those people who distrust newspapers (or who do not read them), do not belong to educational or civic organizations, and cannot follow complex technical and legal material.

The two newspapers, however, bore the chief burden of the proponents' campaign.[28] It has already been noted that the newspapers covered the planning and preparatory sessions of the charter commission. They also participated in the speaking campaign and wrote stories, feature articles, and question-and-answer columns about the plan. Pictures were also printed showing the poor state of waste disposal and traffic control in an effort to suggest that metropolitan government would alleviate these problems.

Much has been made of the fact that both papers supported consolidated government. Only very rarely have the *Banner* and the *Tennessean* agreed on controversial political questions, and the fact that they both vigorously supported Metro aroused suspicion among some residents of Davidson County. Indeed, this writer was assured several times in his own interviewing of voters that when both papers are on the same side "something's fishy."

A large number of the area's civic clubs also supported Metro.

26. Quoted in David Grubbs, *op. cit.,* p. 255.
27. See also Daniel J. Elazar, *op. cit.,* pp. 43, 44.
28. A few individual speakers also made strenuous efforts. The Mayor, the County Judge, many of the planners, and some reporters fall in this select category. So do a number of young lawyers who formed the official speakers' bureau.

So did numerous PTA groups and members. Such groups, however, tend by their very nature to be populated by more serious-minded readers and meeting-frequenters. Daniel J. Elazar suggests that by directing the speaking campaign toward civic clubs, the PTA, and informal neighborhood gatherings, most of them in the upper-income areas, the proponents lulled themselves into a "false sense of security." Speakers at such gatherings were almost invariably confronted by sympathetic and friendly audiences, and they thus tended to feel that all was well.[29]

But all was not well, despite the fact that there did not seem to be any real opposition throughout most of the campaign. While the supporters were "explaining" the charter the opponents bided their time. Just prior to the vote they launched what has since been characterized (by the newspapers) as a "massive scare campaign." No holds were barred, and the fact that their thrust was made at so late a date made it all the more difficult to parry (although it also reduced the probabilities that many people would hear about it).

The opponents' effort was directed almost exclusively toward the county; for the city, as Mayor West's stronghold, was thought to be lost. Thousands of handbills were circulated about higher taxes, the absence of services for the foreseeable future, the city's newspapers, and Nashville's mayor who they suggested hoped to take county residents into the city and thereby gain dictatorial powers over them. Other allegations included the likelihood of extending liquor sales to the suburbs under Metro—an unwelcome prospect for many of the area's church-goers—and various allegations about "socialism" and "big government."

In addition, many Negroes were apprised of the fact that consolidation would dilute their city-centered voting power.

Perhaps even more important were the activities of the so-called "private politicians" and county's subscription fire, police, and garbage-collection units. These organizations existed over most

29. Daniel J. Elazar, *op. cit.*, pp. 41, 42.

of the fringe area outside the City of Nashville, and, largely out of fear for their jobs, they constituted a ready-made, grass-roots, door-to-door, opposition "machine."[30] Constables, deputy sheriffs, and many magistrates joined in.

Financial support came from a very few rich individuals who opposed the plan from the beginning,[31] from gamblers and bootleggers who feared a change in the status quo, and from five-hundred-dollar assessments levied on each private fire and police chief. Not all of the latter contributed, but many did.[32]

Other opposition activities included full-page ads in the newspapers and radio jingles stressing the inevitability of tax increases under Metro. One newspaper ad read, "Your home will be encumbered with a new debt if metropolitan government is voted in."

THE 1958 VOTE AND WHY IT FAILED

On June 17, 1958, the voters of Nashville and Davidson County rejected the proposed Metro charter. As its opponents intended, the county area outside the city voted substantially against consolidation (see Table III, p. 148 of the section entitled "Additional Tables"). The City of Nashville, however, voted strongly in favor of the charter, though in a light turnout. Its ratios, in fact, were approximately the reverse of those of the county, that is, 3 to 2 as against 2 to 3.

The only three county districts that supported the 1958 charter (the Seventh, Eighth, and Sixteenth) contained the wealthiest communities in Davidson County: Oak Hill, Belle Meade, Forest Hills, and the Hillwood–West Meade Area adjoining Belle Meade on the west. The percentage for the charter in the Hillwood area was 53, whereas the Seventh District, containing Belle Meade,

30. It is doubtful, however, that many of them had access to the "door" in the upper-income suburbs. But these are not as populous as the lower-income areas.

31. Most of the wealthy presumably supported Metro; a few presumably did not. It was rumored that most of the latter were "ultraconservatives," but the author uncovered no evidence for this.

32. Daniel J. Elazar, *op. cit.*, p. 86.

voted 72.3 per cent and the Sixteenth, containing Oak Hill, voted 67.1 per cent.

The county areas that voted heavily against the charter included Donelson, Madison, Inglewood, and virtually every rural district in the county. (See map, facing p. 18.) Among the latter was the Tenth District, containing the City of Goodlettsville (then unincorporated but soon to incorporate). The Tenth District voted 90.7 per cent against the charter. The two districts containing the community of Donelson voted 68.1 per cent and 82.5 per cent against it; comparable figures for Madison and Inglewood were 73.9 per cent and 53.6 per cent respectively.

Thus the voters rang down the curtain, in rather convincing fashion, on the 1958 consolidation proposal. Since then many have tried to account for this outcome. What happened? The proponents seemed to have had on their side the preponderance of community leaders, plus both metropolitan newspapers. The political and the business elites both appeared to be solidly behind the proposal. Even the most cautious student of community power structure could not help being impressed. And yet the results speak for themselves.

No one has undertaken through survey research to uncover voter attitudes at the time of the 1958 referendum.[33] In the absence of such a study, one can only cite the interpretations and analyses of some of the observers of the 1958 referendum. One of the most commonly accepted interpretations places primary blame for the failure on the proponents' campaign. David Grubbs, for example, has said that the most obvious weakness in the campaign was the lack of a grass-roots, door-to-door, approach.[34]

This evaluation of the 1958 campaign is heavily supported by

33. For a study of the attitudes of local government legislators, however, see David A. Booth and Daniel R. Grant, "Metro and Local Government Legislators," in *Metropolitics: The Nashville Consolidation*, ed. David A. Booth (East Lansing, Michigan: Institute for Community Development and Services, 1963). Most of this study deals with the 1958 referendum, but the last section, written immediately after the 1962 vote, is on the 1962 referendum.

34. David Grubbs, *op. cit.*, p. 374.

other observers of the Nashville scene.[35] In addition, the members
of the Nashville Charter Commission, when asked what caused
the defeat of the proposed charter, expressed a common theme—
"A grass-roots, door-to-door, neighborhood procharter campaign
was lacking."[36] The election figures themselves, moreover, lend
considerable plausibility to this analysis, for it was probably in
the (heavily pro-Metro) upper-income (Seventh, Eighth, and
Sixteenth) civil districts that the highest percentages of people
also tended to read newspapers, attend meetings, and otherwise
seek to be informed. Assuming that income and education are
objective indicators of the same phenomenon (sometimes called
"class status"), the type of campaign waged by the proponents of
consolidation in 1958 appears to have reached upper-status
people in sufficient numbers; but others were apparently not
reached in sufficient numbers.

Thus Grubbs found a positive relationship between economic
status and procharter sentiment.

Within the central city, however, the economic interpretation
appears somewhat suspect. It is true that the highest vote for
the charter was attained in the ward (the fourth) having a population most similar in education and income to the Seventh, Eighth,
and Sixteenth civil districts. But several very low-income wards
also went substantially for the charter. One, the third, was heavily
if not predominantly Negro at the time of the 1958 referendum,[37]
thus indicating (though imperfectly) a comparatively low-income
and low-education level. It supported Metro by 65.7 per
cent. The Fifth Ward also contained a very high percentage of
Negroes, if not a majority, and many low-income whites as well,

35. Among those endorsing it are Robert Horton, Director of Research
of the city and county Planning Commissions; Amon Evans, Publisher
the Nashville *Tennessean*; Dr. James Phythyon, Civic Committee on Public Education; James Roberson, Co-ordinator, 1962 Citizens for Better
Government Committee; Mrs. J. D. Sanders, Women's Division 1962 Citizens Committee; and Dr. Vivian Henderson, Economics Professor, Fisk
University.

36. Grubbs, *op. cit.*, p. 353.

37. Daniel J. Elazar, *op. cit.*, p. 68.

but it too supported Metro, albeit by a narrow 50.7 per cent majority. The Sixth and Seventh wards, both in East Nashville, contained and still contain a number of Negroes and a preponderance of low-income whites. Both voted for the 1958 charter.

Clearly, central city wards and county civil districts displayed markedly different voting behavior, despite substantially similar economic and educational characteristics. Consequently, variables other than educational and economic ones must have been at work. Without getting deeply involved in a discussion of the causes underlying the 1958 vote, which is not the purpose of the present study, several additional variables demand our attention.

One of the most important possibilities is the racial factor. There is some prima facie support in the aggregate voting returns for the contention that the racial factor was important. Thus the two city wards that voted against the charter were predominantly Negro while the all-white wards, not only in the city but outside as well, voted heavily for the charter.[38]

Grubbs found that the Negroes on the whole did not favor the charter and that, the higher the proportion of Negroes the less the support for the charter.[39]

To turn to other variables, it is quite possible that the city administration, or its "machine," as some would have it, was able in 1958 to achieve a very considerable vote for the position espoused by its director, Mayor West. Nor is this surprising in view of the large numbers of city employees, particularly firemen and policemen, with contacts in virtually every nook and cranny of the old city. City councilmen friendly to Mayor West also had their own precinct organizations in many cases.

The mayor himself, as might be expected, expressed a somewhat different view of the pro-Metro activities in the City of Nashville. Success was due, as he saw it, to a greater explanatory effort on the part of the city. "If the same effort had been put

38. Obviously, a variety of factors *could* account for these results, but in this section factors other than the racial ones are omitted.
39. See David Grubbs, *op. cit.*, pp. 358, 359.

forth in the county by way of explanation as in the city, we might
have had a different outcome."[40] In any case, the majority of
those voting in the seven wards of the old city (before the large
annexations of 1960) voted the Mayor's position in both the
1958 and 1962 referenda, changing sides as he did.

Another factor that might have been at work in 1958 was the
time-honored cleavage between central city and county outside.
Many voters in the latter portion of Davidson County doubtless
held attitudes widely thought to be typical of such areas. When
applied to the 1958 referendum, this interpretation holds that
the "no" vote in the county was an anticity vote (and an anti-
Mayor vote), with the whole spectrum of attitudes that this
entails.

Daniel Elazar has suggested still another way to account for
the failure of the 1958 charter — that the most fundamental difference between the areas that voted for Metro and those that
voted against it was their residents' "frame of reference." Two
wholly separate outlooks were involved, he argues, and they cor-
respond roughly to attitudes attributed by Robert K. Merton to
"locals" and "cosmopolitans."[41] This concept involves the way
people view the community around them, their attitude toward
their more immediate environment. In the present case, "cosmopolitans" were viewed as having a considerably wider sense of
community than "locals." The former were thought to be less
oriented toward their immediate area, whether neighborhood,
suburb, or rural community, and more oriented toward greater
Nashville. They thought of themselves first as Nashvillians.

The locals' frame of reference was just the opposite. They
were thought to be neighborhood- or local community-oriented,
to possess little sense of a greater community, and to be
typically unaware of community problems and local government
issues. "Locals seem predominant at lower-class, lower middle-

40. Ben West, "Statement to the Davidson County Legislative Delegation," Nashville, January 11, 1961.
41. Robert K. Merton, *Social Theory and Social Structure* (Glencoe,
Illinois: The Free Press, 1957).

class, and upper upper-class levels while cosmopolitans seem to predominate at the middle and upper middle-class and the lower upper-class levels."[42]

Elazar undertakes in his case study to classify most of the wards, districts, and communities in Davidson County as being either predominantly "local" or "cosmopolitan" in character. He does this on the basis of descriptive comments furnished by the forty-three politicians, political activists, and key observers he interviewed, supplemented by demographic data. Well over eighty per cent of his respondents accepted the idea of differences in frames of reference of the two groupings. Elazar states, however, that only survey research techniques can properly determine the accuracy of this classification.[43]

Such sociological classifications are clearly a step removed from the reasons voters actually employ to decide one way or the other. They may well display classically local or cosmopolitan frames of reference, but they tend to vote in terms of taxes, services, personalities, or belief systems. In addition to the variables discussed above, we thus must also note the following possible sources of opposition to the 1958 charter: fear of higher taxes under a consolidated government; general ignorance and apathy; fear of centralized government; suspicion of newspaper support and that of the area's "big wheels"; disbelief that consolidation would improve services.

Fear of higher taxes with consolidation is regarded by Elazar as the "biggest single issue."[44] Among those Nashville-area voters concerned about higher taxes, it is safe to say that insufficient numbers were placated by the explanations and promises of Metro's proponents—especially, no doubt, when the same proponents were widely mistrusted anyway.

Voter ignorance and apathy is a subject that is widely treated in the literature. Nashville and Davidson County doubtless di-

42. Daniel J. Elazar, *op. cit.*, p. 10.
43. *Ibid.*, p. 9.
44. *Ibid.*, p. 100.

verge but little from a national pattern revealing considerable ignorance and indifference on the part of the electorate, particularly in matters of local government and politics.[45] Thus the 1958 vote saw but a 34.5 per cent turnout of registered voters in the area.

Regarding the "fear of centralized government," it should be noted that Nashville and Davidson County contain fairly large numbers of people variously known as "ultraconservatives," "ultrarightists," and so on. Nashville, in fact, is said to be one of the strongholds of the John Birch Society. As noted earlier, charges of "socialism" and "big government" were widespread in the 1958 campaign and perhaps convinced many people to vote against Metro.

For many in the area, the Nashville newspapers are simply not a trusted source of opinion and information. Suspicion of the area's "big wheels"—the leading lights of the business, financial and political communities—is similarly prevalent among some voters.

Disbelief that consolidation would bring the services lacking in some areas is self-explanatory. In 1962 the author was told by numerous county voters that city-type services would never be extended to them, or at least not for many years.

CONCLUSIONS

The 1958 Nashville referendum appeared to be much like other referenda on governmental integration. The actual proposal was put forward by such typically reformist groups as a taxpayers' association, a chamber of commerce study committee, a special "community services commission" established by private

45. See Robert E. Lane, *Political Life* (Glencoe, Illinois: The Free Press, 1959) for an excellent overview of the problem and a thorough bibliography of the specifics. See also Edward McDill and Jeanne Clare Ridley, "Status, Anomia, Political Alienation, and Political Participation," *American Journal of Sociology*, LXVIII (September 1962), 205–213. The latter study was conducted in the Nashville area and serves to support the proposition that large numbers of Nashville-area voters are ignorant and apathetic.

act of the state legislature, and by city and county planners. It was then supported by numerous civic associations, by businessmen and young lawyers, and by the central city mayor in a largely amateurish, upper-class, good-government campaign. The mayor's machine, however, took an active part also. The opposition concentrated on the county area and stressed such issues as higher taxes and city dictatorship.

The outcome was a typical "yes" vote in the city and a "no" vote outside. Similar results occurred in the Louisville area in 1956, the Macon area in 1960, and the Richmond area in 1961.

There was, in short, nothing very different about the Nashville referendum of 1958.

6

ANNEXATION AND CITY-COUNTY
DISSENSION: 1958–1962

FOLLOWING the defeat of the 1958 consolidation proposal, the City of Nashville moved to annex county
territory and in so doing provided the next link in our
story, for the resulting annexations aroused emotions that were to
play an important part in the 1962 referendum. It is therefore to
the subject of annexation that we now turn.

Of the four major cities in Tennessee, only one—Memphis—
shows a record of expansion commensurate with its physical
growth, and this was due primarily to the fact that Boss Crump
could accomplish annexations by private acts of the state legislature through his control of the Shelby County legislative delegation. Nashville, Knoxville, and Chattanooga all experienced long
periods without any substantial annexations of county territory.

Thus in the Nashville area no large-scale annexations took
place from 1929 to 1958. However, in 1958, two days after the
consolidation proposal was defeated, the city annexed seven
square miles of industrial territory, without a referendum, on the
grounds that the area was already receiving city services and that
industries as such cannot vote in any case. The city stood to
benefit financially from this addition, of course, and the West
administration took the position that it was essential to com-
pensate for the shrinkage of taxable land within the city.[1] The

1. In 1958–1959, it was estimated that close to 40 per cent of the city's
total real estate was tax-exempt because it was owned or operated for
governmental, charitable, or religious purposes. The city faced, in addi-

annexation was to become effective January 1, 1959, but a month before that date some fifty-three businessmen filed suit challenging its validity.

At about the same time Mayor West was quoted in the *Banner* as stating that he would call for a referendum in any broad residential annexation. It was widely assumed that such residential annexations would follow.

Then in August 1959 the city passed an ordinance levying a wheel tax on all motor vehicles using the streets of Nashville for thirty days or more. The tax amounted to ten dollars, and it raised an immediate uproar among county residents. It was charged, to begin with, that this was "taxation without representation." Nor did it add to the popularity of the city administration that the "green-sticker law," as it came to be called because the required stickers were green, went through three council readings and became law within a week. The mayor, on the other hand, contended that the city needed additional revenue and that such an auto tax was not a bad way to get it. It was, after all, better than additional property levies.

Many people, however, simply refused to buy the required green stickers before the deadline, in part because they doubted that such a measure could be enforced. How, for example, could the police check on the number of days one "used" the city streets?

The fact that many car owners were ignoring the ordinance in turn angered those who had paid the ten dollars. According to the Nashville newspapers, city officials were then subjected to a storm of complaints from such people. City councilmen subsequently called for strict enforcement.

A sudden police crackdown followed. The police began arresting car owners and hauling them up before City Judge Andrew Doyle. Violators were not given traffic tickets; they were arrested, taken to court, and fined fifty dollars.

---

tion, the problem of an increasing Negro population with its attendant decrease in tax receipts. Finally, the city received little return for the many services it provided to suburbanites who worked in the city.

Then the sparks really began to fly. The *Tennessean* daily ran stories telling of citizens being nabbed and hauled into court "like common criminals," sometimes even in the paddy wagon. A few motorists claimed that they were arrested while driving someone else's car. The *Tennessean* stated editorially that no man ought to be carried off to headquarters, booked and jailed for such a minor offense as failure to buy a ten-dollar sticker.[2]

It was not long, however, before delinquent motorists began flocking to city hall to purchase their stickers. In a short while the arrests tapered off and the *Tennessean* ceased its crusade.

Nevertheless, the green-sticker episode left a residue of ill will among county residents. Many found it hard to forget the manner in which the ordinance was "railroaded" through the council and the way it was enforced. Nor did the recent industrial annexation (still pending in the courts) contribute to the popularity of the West administration among county voters. The fact that a large residential annexation was in the air further compounded the animosity.[3]

Meanwhile the proponents of Metro were anxious to have another try at it. They hoped to establish a new charter commission, and early in 1960 they managed to achieve a favorable vote in the county quarterly court. The city council, however, voted against a new charter commission proposal, thus thwarting Metro aspirations for the time being.

In the wake of this action, a bill was introduced in the city council to annex without referendum some forty-two square miles and 82,000 persons.[4] In an "unusual burst of speed"[5] the council passed the measure on three readings and overrode a veto by the Mayor (which enabled him to claim some kind of adherence

2. The Nashville *Tennessean,* December 11, 1959.

3. See Chapter Nine for an indication of county voter attitudes as revealed by the author's interviews.

4. The councilmen introducing this proposal were Aubrey D. Gillem, the Mayor's floor leader, and Charles Bramwell. Both were destined to widespread popular association with this annexation.

5. Daniel R. Grant and Lee S. Greene, "Survey, Dust, Action," *National Civic Review,* L (October, 1961), 470.

to his earlier promise not to annex a residential area without a referendum) all within the month of April 1960. Interpretations of the mayor's veto vary, but opponents point out that the mayor's own floor leader, A. D. Gillem, both proposed the measure and led the move to override the veto. The *Tennessean*, of course, pounced on this theme with gusto. But Mayor West and his supporters denied that the veto was motivated by anything other than genuine opposition to the proposed annexation,[6] and they also argued—somewhat inconsistently—that the annexation was a carefully planned undertaking. Nonetheless, "it seems clear that the veto would not have been overridden without an informal 'green light' from the mayor to his normally controlling majority on the city council."[7]

The annexation was immediately challenged in the courts.

Despite statements by the city administration, this whole episode was widely regarded by West's critics as a naked subterfuge and an example of the sort of chicanery and cynicism of which the mayor was (allegedly) capable. The *Tennessean* did its part to further this interpretation, and indeed it mounted an increasingly vehement attack. The *Banner*, however, defended both the mayor and the annexations. Its local political reporter, Dick Battle, emphasized that Metro had already been turned down by the voters and that the wisest course was to turn to other means. He stressed the announced determination of the city to extend city services to the annexed areas as rapidly as possible, and he defended the procedure of first annexing seven square miles of industrial and commercial territory on the ground that the residential areas could not provide sufficient revenue to meet the cost of their own municipal services.[8]

Battle later told this author that once West had committed himself to the annexation plans he (West) "could not go back

6. Gillem told this author that West felt obliged to protect his stated public position, but that he (West) did not *know* it would pass. Gillem also stated that West gave him no instructions. Interview, December 22, 1962.

7. Daniel R. Grant and Lee S. Greene, *op. cit.*, p. 470.

8. The Nashville *Banner*, May 6, 1960.

and support Metro." The mayor was also convinced, according to Battle, that the people who were trying to revive Metro "were doing so primarily to defeat him," and that in 1958 he would have been elected Metro mayor. In any new Metro government, however, West believed that he would be out in the cold because of annexation, the wheel tax, and "vicious newspaper opposition."[9]

West himself, however, told this author that his main reasons for opposing Metro were that the 1962 charter was weaker than the 1958 charter, and that it was being used by local elements, particularly the *Tennessean*, to oust him from office after their failure to get his ear and dictate to him.

Whatever the true source of West's opposition, it became clear soon after the first annexation—if it was not already clear—that West would oppose any effort to revive Metro, and that the *Banner* would support him.[10]

It is plausible, of course, that the *Tennessean* did decide to get rid of West despite his liberal record on such issues as urban renewal and state legislative apportionment because they could not exert much influence over him. In an interview with this author, however, Amon C. Evans, Publisher of the *Tennessean*, denied that this was the case; but he emphasized that the pro-Metro people were fortunate to have the person of Ben West to attack. (Interview, November 26, 1962).

City Finance Director Joe Torrence told this author a story which lends some support to this "if you can't join 'em (as an influencing force), lick 'em" interpretation of the *Tennessean*'s

9. Interview with Dick Battle, December 13, 1962.

10. One of the more interesting paradoxes in the newspaper alignment derives from the fact that the generally liberal *Tennessean* supported the more conservative politician, Briley, and the generally conservative *Banner* supported the more liberal politician, West.

The reason for this situation is not entirely clear. It is true that West was once a reporter on the *Banner* (according to Dick Battle), and that in 1951 the *Banner* supported West in his first campaign for mayor (while the *Tennessean* supported the incumbent), but these facts would not seem to amount to a full explanation.

behavior. According to Torrence, the advocates of annexation asked the *Tennessean* to get behind annexation after Metro failed in 1958, and "they" replied that they were tempted to do so but that if they did, and if annexation were politically successful, they would never get West out of office. (Interview, November 29, 1962).

Needless to say, none of this constitutes conclusive proof of the "if we can't join 'em, lick 'em" thesis.

On August 19, 1960, in any case, chancery court upheld the annexation of forty-two square miles by the City of Nashville. The timing of this ruling was something of a surprise, for the court had not yet ruled on the *other* Nashville annexation, then two years old. Editorially the *Tennessean* asked whether the Metro threat, which had been disposed of by the city council, caused the speedy decision.

At the end of the year (December 30, 1960), and after a delay of two years, chancery court also upheld the previous annexation of seven square miles of industrial and commercial property. Both rulings were appealed to the state supreme court.

Then in March of 1961 the supreme court affirmed chancery court's decree upholding the residential annexation. In its decision the court took judicial notice of the 1952 report of the Community Services Commission, a report which had, of course, recommended large-scale annexation.

Ironically, this decision of the state supreme court came just at the time that the Davidson County legislative delegation was trying to resurrect Metro by a new method—private legislation. An even greater irony, perhaps, derives from the action of the state legislature—also prior to the court's ruling—to require that future annexations include a definite plan for serving annexed residents and a definite schedule of the plan's fulfillment. There was no such plan in Nashville in 1960, although Gillem and Bramwell did work with the planning commission for some time.[11]

11. At least one planner interviewed by the author denied that there was any genuine plan at all, not to mention the sort required by the above statute.

Within six months after the court decision nine new city councilmen had been elected, and bond issues had been approved to
finance the new services. General obligation bonds in the amount
of 5.5 million dollars were issued to finance the extension of trunk
sewers into the annexed areas, nearly all of which suffered from
the acute septic ills common to Nashville's suburbs. On June 1,
1960, the *Banner* ran the following bold headline: "City Population 253,937." Doubtless many people in the metropolitan area
looked upon this aspect of annexation as its most important feature.

All was not harmonious, however. Annexation was beginning
to produce some friction between the city and the county. Furthermore, the *Tennessean*, in its dual role of Metro supporter and
West antagonist, played up every incident that might further the
causes for which it stood.

One of the first conflicts to flare into the open concerned the
roads in the annexed area. Davidson County, shortly after annexation, abandoned plans to improve such roads, and the Chairman
of the County Highway Commission announced that the county
could not afford to spend its money on city streets.[12]

In the end, however, annexation was upheld by the courts and
the responsibility for street and road maintenance fell to the city.

It is noteworthy also that just prior to the Metro vote the city
launched a rather extensive road-repair project both in the old
city and in the newly annexed areas. This move was widely interpreted by the West administration's opponents (and/or the
proponents of consolidated government) as being motivated by
"political considerations."

Of course the whole question of municipal services was of real
concern to many residents of the annexed areas. It is not surprising that they wanted to know about their city services and when
they could expect to receive them. Many were skeptical that they
would receive anything very extensive in the way of new services.

12. The Nashville *Tennessean*, May 7, 1960.

On March 21, 1961, however, the city started police, fire, and garbage collection services in the annexed area. Some 150 additional policemen and 70 additional firemen were taken on, and four new fire stations were planned.

Many residents of the annexed areas hoped especially that they would eventually receive sewerage "now that they were in the city." They were destined to be disappointed, despite the fact that sewer studies were begun as far back as 1955. Even so, the city did make some progress on the sewer problem after the annexation. It sold 5.5 million dollars worth of general obligation bonds, retained an engineering firm to draw up a detailed sewer design, and—just prior to the Metro vote in 1962—started putting down some trunk lines.

Another area in which city-county friction developed was taxation. In August 1961 County Tax Assessor Clifford Allen asked chancery court to decide whether property taxes in the annexed areas should be based on the county rate for unincorporated places or the (lower) city tax rate. At that time the city rate was $2.33 per $100 of assessed valuation, the county rate was $2.78.[13] Allen stated that the tax levy passed by the county court, prior to annexation, required him to use the higher rate for these areas, although he personally thought that this was discriminatory.

On September 22, 1961, chancery court ruled that the residents of the annexed areas had to pay the $2.78 county rate for the following year. The Chancellor based his ruling on the fact that assessments were made prior to the effective date of annexation. Allen commented that he still thought the tax wrong, both morally and legally.[14]

Just prior to Metro's adoption, finally, Judge Briley announced that the county government, caught in a financial squeeze by

13. The difference was caused by a 23-cent district school tax to amortize costs of school construction financed by bonds issued on property outside the city, and a 22-cent road tax to finance road maintenance outside the city. See the Nashville *Tennessean*, August 8, 1961.

14. *Ibid.*, September 22, 1961.

annexation, might be forced to raise the rate for unincorporated areas to $3.00 (from $2.78).

The residents of the annexed area were, it is safe to say, uniformly displeased about their new taxes. Many who were making monthly payments on a home and living on a tight budget found the increase a genuine burden. Anticity attitudes doubtless came easy to such people, particularly if they were already inclined to accept the anti-West forces' interpretation of means employed to annex them.

Still another source of city-county friction was the schools in the annexed area. While the annexation ordinance was still being considered, a controversy arose concerning the transportation of pupils to schools in these areas. In April 1960 the county school board announced that it would not haul pupils in any areas annexed to the city.

Two months later (after the annexation had been completed) the school controversy was in full bloom. Judge Briley charged that the whole mess resulted from the fact that the annexation had not been carefully planned. Mayor West denied it. Parents and teachers displayed considerable displeasure generally, and many called for an early agreement on the transfer of schools in the annexed areas.

A step was taken in this direction when on July 6, 1960, Nashville and Davidson County school boards adopted a school transfer pact. The agreement spelled out the steps to be taken in the transfer of the schools. In the meantime the proponents of consolidated government had gotten through the state assembly a private act to create another Metro charter commission. On August 17, 1961, this act was made effective in a special election.

Then in September, 1961, the school controversy flared once more when the City of Nashville offered the county 6.4 million dollars for the twenty-two schools in the recently annexed areas. The Davidson County School Board, however, announced that it wanted to keep four of the twenty-two schools in the annexed areas, including one high school, because a large percentage of the students attending those schools lived in areas still outside the corporate limits of Nashville. A month later the county school board rejected Nashville's offer of 6.4 million dollars for the schools in the annexed areas. The board held out for a price covering the replacement value of the schools, which it figured at more than 11 million dollars.

Then in November the county board of education voted to fight in court to continue operation of the four county schools in question. The resulting suit between the City of Nashville and Davidson County dragged on for months.

At the same time another conflict was growing over the best way to select a school board under metropolitan government, should it be adopted. To appoint or to elect: that was the question. The city superintendent took a stand for a mayor-appointed board, the county superintendent for an elected board. The existing boards, both city and county, went on record as opposing the popular election of school boards in a consolidated government.[15] The area's educators, however, spoke out strongly for an elected board.

This controversy over the selection of a school board under metropolitan government eventually spilled over into the deliberations of the Metro charter commission, which was established in the fall of 1961.

15. *Ibid.,* October 20, 1961.

THE 1962 CHARTER COMMISSION

B EFORE considering the charter commission and its deliberations, the following chronological summary of the Nashville story, up to establishment of the new charter commission, is offered:

1950—The election to the county judgeship of Beverly Briley.

1951—The election of Ben West as Nashville Mayor.

1952—The report of the Community Services Commission on the problems of metropolitan Nashville.

1953—The amendment to the Tennessee Constitution permitting the general assembly to provide for the consolidation of any or all governmental functions vested in municipalities or counties.

1955—The statute authorizing municipalities to annex county territory by ordinance.

1955—The strategy sessions of Hand, Hawkins, Horton, and Grant.

1956—The "Plan of Metropolitan Government for Nashville and Davidson County" recommending immediate annexation but placing greater emphasis on a comprehensive plan for city-county consolidation.

1957—The enabling act providing for consolidations in counties having a population of 200,000 or more.

1958—The establishment of the charter commission, the drafting of the charter, and the charter's defeat.

1958-1962—Annexation and city-county dissension.

Early in 1960 the proponents of Metro managed to get a favorable vote for creating a new charter commission in the county quarterly court, but no such favorable vote came from the city council. Indeed, it was clear that the city council had annexation on its mind and was not ready to support the creation of a Metro charter commission. That which followed—a large residential annexation with city-county tension in its wake—has been considered above. In the meantime county elections were held, and the candidates for the quarterly court who had been supporting another try at consolidation led the field. In the small suburban City of Berry Hill, moreover, anti-Metro magistrate Ewing Clouse was defeated by a large majority. The mayor-endorsed candidate for sheriff was also defeated—by a political novice who had indicated his support for Metro.

These elections were widely interpreted as marking the turn of the popularity tide against Mayor West. The *Tennessean* commented editorially, "The mayor's political machine . . . gasped and conked out under the onslaught of independent votes."[1]

When it became apparent that the annexations would not be struck down by the courts, the movement to try "one government" again got under way. The proponents know full well, of course, that under existing state law they would not be able to create a new charter commission. The city council stood squarely in their path. Consequently the proponents sought to amend the general act of 1957 to provide a second or alternative method for creating a charter commission. Their strategy was to amend the general act to permit the establishment of a charter commission in a manner prescribed by private act, as well as by similar resolution of the two governing bodies.

The Davidson County legislative delegation did not encounter any serious difficulties in getting the general assembly to go along with the proposed amendment. This was because the new provision was to be permissive (not mandatory) and because it was thought to apply mostly to Davidson County.

1. The Nashville *Tennessean*, April 3, 1960.

On March 9, 1961, the desired amendment was enacted[2] and a week later the Davidson County legislative delegation proposed a private act creating a charter commission for Nashville and Davidson County. On March 16, 1961, this measure also was enacted into law.[3]

This important private act creating a new charter body came into being in part because the Davidson County legislative delegation had gone to the General Assembly virtually committed to giving the people another chance to vote on Metro. In the months preceding the August 1960 primary, Metro had been made a campaign issue, and the members of the Davidson County delegation pledged themselves to secure for the people another chance to vote on it.

When the legislature met in January, however, the twelve-man Davidson County legislative delegation was split over the question of a new charter commission. Anti-Metro interests were seeking to persuade some of them to oppose the private act, and three were wavering. After some pressure from pro-Metro interests, however, two of them came around and agreed to support the private act. But the third representative altogether refused to support it. Nevertheless, the Assembly went ahead and passed the private act over the dissent of one representative from the area in question. Why it took this wholly unprecedented action is not entirely clear, but it is certain that a considerable amount of spade work in the form of trading support was done before the formal vote.

Under the Tennessee Constitution, however, such a private act is not valid until approved either by local legislative bodies or by a majority of the voters in the jurisdictions affected—in this case separate majorities in the county outside the city and in the city. The first method was obviously out of the question. It was

2. Chapter 199, Public Acts of 1961.
3. Chapter 408, Private Acts of 1961. Metro opponents subsequently argued that this method for creating the charter commission was unconstitutional.

therefore provided in the private act itself that an election be
held on August 17, 1961, for purposes of validating (or rejecting)
the creation of a metropolitan charter commission.

The election was held, and in a light vote the city and county
voters supported the creation of a new charter commission. There
had apparently been a change of heart among at least some of the
voters in the county.

	For	Against
Inside the city	11,096	3,730
County outside the city	7,324	3,848

Source: The Nashville *Tennessean*, August 18, 1961.

The campaign preceding the charter commission referendum
was important because it saw the formation of a new citizens'
organization to fight for the passage of Metro. The group sponsored a series of public meetings in various parts of the county to
explain the charter referendum and to win support for Metro
generally. The opposition, on the other hand, made no real effort
to block the formation of a new charter commission, although
some "scare" literature was distributed.

Eight of the ten members of the new commission were named
in the private act and were the same persons that served on the
1958 commission. These were Carmack Cochran, a prominent
attorney and civic leader who was chairman of the 1958 commission; Miss Rebecca Thomas, an attorney who had served as
commission secretary in 1958; Cecil Branstetter, an attorney
frequently representing labor interests; R. N. Chenault, principal
of an elementary school in a lower-income district; K. Harlan
Dodson, Jr., an attorney and former state senator; G. S. Meadors,
a retired Negro druggist; Victor S. Johnson, president of a large
business concern and past president of the Nashville Chamber of
Commerce; and Z. Alexander Looby, a popular Negro attorney
and city councilman. Edwin F. Hunt was retained as legal counsel
to the charter body, a position which he had filled with distinction
in 1958.

Two charter commission vacancies had occurred since 1958,

and the private act provided that these be filled by appointment by the mayor and the county judge. Mayor West appointed Joe E. Torrence, the City Finance Director, and Judge Briley appointed Charles Warfield a thirty-six-year-old attorney who had been active in circles seeking to revive Metro.

The quickest glance at the members of the charter commission indicates that a variety of viewpoints and interests was represented, even though six of the ten were attorneys. There were of course two Negroes on the commission, one of whom, Mr. Looby, carried immense prestige among members of his race. As for the liberal-conservative composition of the charter body, the *Tennessean* characterized Branstetter, Torrence, and Warfield as "liberals" and noted that Carmack Cochran, although calling himself a conservative, was favorably disposed toward certain local programs such as governmental reform and urban renewal which were generally regarded as liberal.

Branstetter was considered a spokesman for the labor point of view. Joe Torrence was naturally considered the West administration's spokesman, having been its Finance Director for some time.

Victor Johnson, of course, was the obvious representative of the business community, although attorneys Harlan Dodson and Carmack Cochran also were regarded as conservative, business-oriented gentlemen. Cochran had been president of the Nashville Chamber of Commerce, and Dodson had championed the causes of management as a state senator.

Miss Thomas, a well-known woman attorney and civic leader, described herself as a political moderate interested especially in the conduct of fair public hearings by the commission. Chenault was regarded as the spokesman for the area's educators, a group evidently regarded very highly by the community.

DELIBERATIONS OF THE CHARTER COMMISSION
AND THE RESULTING CHARTER

The new charter commission took as its starting point the 1958 charter, and it was required to operate with essentially the same enabling act as a guide. As a result, much of its work and the issues that confronted it were similar to those of 1958. The major issues were once again the disposition of the schools, representation on the Metro council (including the question of Negro representation), the nature of the two taxing districts, and the provisions relating to pensions, civil service, and other employee matters. The resulting document was not very different from the 1958 charter, although just how different was a question about which Metro's proponents and opponents disagree sharply. The differences between the two charters are taken up below.

Schools. In October the first in a series of meetings on the education section of the consolidation charter was held. The meetings were sponsored by the Civic Committee on Public Education in co-operation with the city and county PTA councils, the Citizens for Better Government,[4] and the education subcommittee of the charter commission. During October and November meetings were held in various high schools, including two Negro schools, throughout the county.

It was not long before these meetings turned into open clashes between the advocates of appointment and the advocates of election. At a meeting at Overton High School, in the Oak Hill–Crieve Hall area Joe Torrence and Mr. Robert Bogen, Executive Secretary of the Civic Committee on Public Education, argued rather heatedly. Torrence contended that electing a school board robs the public of the opportunity to have top-quality boards; Bogen replied that in a democratic country the people should have the final voice in who is to run their schools.[5]

A related controversy arose when on November 14, 1961, Mr. Chenault let it be known in a speech before the Rotary Club that the Metro charter might provide for a referendum on the school budget if the legislative body did not approve the budget recommended by the school board. "We are not considering such a

4. The Citizens for Better Government represented the major instrument of the pro-Metro forces. See Chapter Eight.
5. The Nashville *Tennessean,* November 22, 1961.

thing as a separate school taxing district," Chenault said, "but
when the school board has made up its mind after holding public
hearings on the budget, then it should be the responsibility of the
legislative body to approve it."[6]

The charter commission subsequently acted to approve a provision permitting the Metro school board to take its budget to the
voters in a referendum if the Metro council rejected that budget.
The vote was 7 to 2, with only Dodson and Looby opposing.

Then on February 26, 1962, the plenary charter body voted
6 to 4 in favor of a school board appointed by the Metro mayor
and confirmed by a two thirds vote of the Metro council. Each
member of the board was to be selected from one of nine districts.
Thus ended the lengthy and occasionally bitter hassle over the
way to get a "good" board of education under Metro government,
should it be adopted.

Representation in the Legislative Body.   Another concern of
the 1962 charter body was representation in the metropolitan
government legislative body. The specific problems were the size
of the legislative body and the location of district lines.

In October 1961 the commission opened hearings on this
subject. One of the first individuals to be heard was Robert
Lillard, a Negro attorney and city councilman. Lillard urged
that automatic reapportionment be incorporated into the provisions of the Metro charter, and he added that representation
should be based strictly on population rather than on area.[7] It
was understood, of course, that Lillard represented those Negroes
who were concerned lest consolidated government cancel their
growing strength in the old city. If automatic reapportionment
could be achieved, plus representation based strictly upon population, the Negroes' cause would obviously be better served.

Another issue that animated the hearings on legislative representation was the size of the Metro council. It will be recalled
that the 1958 charter provided for a council of 21 members,

6. *Ibid.*, November 15, 1961.
7. *Ibid.*, October 17, 1961.

with 16 chosen from districts and 5 elected at large. This time, however, the commission members felt that public opinion was strongly in favor of a larger council.[8]

Many felt that the charter body was in this instance "playing up" to popular sentiment in order to curry favor. It was charged that they were trying to draw up a charter that would be all things to all people.

The upshot was a council consisting of thirty-five members elected from districts, plus five at-large members. District boundaries were drawn up so that 29 of them were predominantly white and 6 predominantly Negro.[9] (Some Negroes charged, however, that the lines were located in such a manner as to give them six possible representatives *and no more* in the foreseeable future.) Automatic reapportionment was also included in the charter. Article 18, Section 18.06 of the charter provides that the Metropolitan Council must adjust district lines according to population every ten years. If it fails to do so, the "members of the Council shall not receive any further salaries. . . ."

Taxing Districts. The matter of taxing districts was handled by the 1962 charter commission much in the manner of its predecessor. The actual charter provides for a general services district and an urban services district, the latter constituting a municipal corporation. The general services district consists of the total area of the metropolitan government, being also the total area of Davidson County.

The urban services district is made expandable by annexation whenever particular areas of the general services district come to need urban services, and whenever the Metropolitan Government is able to provide such services within a reasonable period, which is not to be greater than one year after ad valorem taxes in the annexed area become due.[10] The extent to which this pro-

---

8. *Ibid.,* October 31, 1961.
9. The actual population ratio in Davidson County was 5 to 1.
10. *Proposed Charter of the Metropolitan Government of Nashville and Davidson County, Tennessee* (Nashville: Metropolitan Government Charter Commission, 1962), p. 1.

vision adequately guaranteed suburban areas that they would not be annexed and taxed at a higher rate without receiving additional services became an issue in the Metro campaign.

The charter also sets up a special three-member "urban council" for the sole purpose of setting the tax rate for the urban services district. Urban council members are those three persons elected to the Metropolitan Council as councilmen-at-large who receive the highest votes and who reside within the area of the urban services district.

Civil Service and Pensions. The charter protects both city and county employees in the enjoyment of existing civil service and pension rights. It also set up a new, actuarially sound pension system for Metropolitan Government employees.[11]

Status of Smaller Cities. Under the 1962 Metro charter the smaller cities in Davidson County, although a part of the general services district, retain their independence. But they are also free to relinquish their charters and merge with the urban services district if they wish.

The Executive Branch. Under the Metro charter, the mayor's term is set at four years, with a three-term limitation. His salary is $25,000 per annum, a $5,000 increase over that of the old mayor of the City of Nashville. He is given the power to appoint all departmental directors and the members of most boards and commissions, in some cases with the consent of two thirds of the Metro council.

Three independently elected fiscal officers are provided, however. They are the metropolitan tax assessor, metropolitan trustee (in Tennessee a tax collections officer), and county court clerk.

Both the Tennessee Constitution and general laws provide that the county court clerk shall be elected, not appointed, for a term

11. Prior to the effective date of Metro there were seven or eight different pension systems. According to the Legal Counsel to Mayor West, many of these were not actuarially sound, but under existing conditions they were *financially* sound. Interview with Clarence McIntyre, Administrative Assistant to Mayor West, December 18, 1962.

of four years. The other two offices were made elective for reasons of political strategy, that is, so as not to alienate the incumbents.

DIFFERENCES BETWEEN THE 1958 AND 1962 CHARTERS

Proponents of Metro contended during the campaign that the two charters were essentially the same, whereas Mayor West contended that the 1962 charter was very unlike the one he had supported in 1958. These rather opposite interpretations of the charter played an important role in the 1962 campaign.

The main differences between provisions of the 1958 and 1962 charters were these: a raise of $5,000 in the mayor's salary, an increase in the size of the metropolitan council from 21 to 41 members, and the provision for a referendum on the school budget should two thirds of the board of education feel that the budget adopted by the Metropolitan Council is inadequate.

SOME COMPLICATIONS

On April 2, 1962, the ten members of the charter commission signed the new charter for a consolidated city-county government. Four days later it was officially filed with the city clerk's office. June 28, 1962, was the date fixed for the referendum.

Then on the 18th of April a suit was filed in chancery court challenging the constitutionality of the charter and the law authorizing it. The persons listed as filing the suit were Robert Lillard, Sam Davis Bell, magistrate and Mayor of Belle Meade, and Lewis Frazer, the former Commissioner of Forest Hills. The defendants were the members of the Davidson County Election Commission, Mayor Ben West, Judge Beverly Briley, State Attorney General George F. McCanless, and Secretary of State Joe C. Carr.

The suit contended that the 1957 general act authorizing the creation of a charter commission to draw up a charter for consolidated government was an unconstitutional delegation of legislative power. It further contended that in actual operation the charter commission went further than the legislature authorized and made numerous unconstitutional changes in the functions of the existing city and county.

On the 25th of April the charter commission voted to defend the charter against the suit challenging it. Edwin F. Hunt, the group's legal counsel, was retained to represent the commission.

Another complication stemmed from Davidson County's construction of a sewer project in the Madison Area. The plan was to develop a sewer district to supply sanitary sewers in the Madison business area. The district was to be operated by the County, the first of its kind in Tennessee. In January 1962 a referendum was held in which the Madison-area voters favored the creation of the district.

The initiation of this sewer district struck fear in the hearts of Metro supporters, who hoped that many suburban voters would see Metro as a way to get the sewers they wanted. As the day of the vote approached, proponents feared that the county sewer district approach would be put forward as an argument that Metro was not needed and that sewers could be gotten by less drastic means than city-council consolidation. This argument was in fact unimportant in the campaign.

8

THE 1962 CAMPAIGN:
ISSUES, INTERESTS AND ACTIVITIES

T HE filing of the consolidation charter on April 6, 1962, marked the start of the formal campaign. Of course there had been a good deal of campaigning already, both for and against the charter.

A part of the reason for the success of the Nashville consolidation must be sought in the nature of the campaign, for it is sometimes suggested that the success or failure of proposed changes in governmental structure rests in large measure with the proponents of change. One of the major concerns below is consequently the activities of Metro's proponents. No less important, of course, is the question of who the proponents (and opponents) were. Another major concern is the issues that were raised in the campaign.

THE PROPONENTS' STRATEGY

In considering the actual strategy of Metro's proponents, one should first be clear as to the persons who devised the strategy. Who were they? The shortest answer to this question is "Silliman Evans, Jr., then Publisher of the *Tennessean*, and James H. Roberson, Co-ordinator of the Citizen's Committee for Better Government." But a more complete answer would have to take into account at least two additional factors.

Evans and Roberson did not direct all the various organizations and individuals who supported Metro, although they did direct the two most important organizations. Even those groups nominally under their influence (for example, groups affiliated with

the Citizens for Better Government) were free to engage in
activities of their own, quite apart from the Evans-Roberson
"strategy."

Their strategy was in part merely an obvious course of action
dictated by a widely shared interpretation of the 1958 failure. To
that extent it was not at all an elaborate and exhaustively pond-
ered "strategy" in the usual sense of the term.

Having made these qualifications, it is possible to talk about a
specific proponent strategy.

Before the August 1961 referendum on the charter commission, Roberson and Evans met in the latter's office at the *Tennessean*. They decided that the 1958 campaign failed primarily
because it lacked an effective pro-Metro, block-by-block, organization. Their conclusion reflected, of course, a widely shared
interpretation.

Roberson and Evans further concluded that the 1958 campaign had not been a "political" campaign but a "community
project" campaign. This was reflected in the effort to sell the
charter as a meritorious reform measure. Roberson felt that a
genuine "political" campaign would demand a "devil" and a
neighborhood-and-block, knock-on-doors, face-to-face canvass
for votes. This was, in fact, Roberson's specialty, for he was
considered a skillful political organizer. Both men felt in addition
that the proponents had used too many big names in 1958 and
that because of the annexation the pro-Metro effort should focus
on the fringe areas just outside the newly annexed areas. They
felt that the annexed areas would "take care of the city" by
providing an enormous anticity vote.

Roberson and Evans knew, as did many other individuals
associated with the pro-Metro cause, that their "strategy" would
serve to raise doubts about the governmental status quo. This is
where the "devil" came in, for they could concentrate their
attacks on Mayor West and his city administration, thus person-
alizing the issue and getting the campaign off the relatively high

level that it assumed in 1958.[1] It was felt that this strategy would reduce the issue to a level everyone could understand and relate to his own experience, directly or indirectly.

This strategy, moreover, was doubly virtuous for the proponents in that it could attract both city and county voters. For county voters, and those in the annexed areas too, Ben West could be presented in terms of the green-sticker tax and the threat of annexation, and for city voters the mere fact of his twelve years in office was certain to interest many in an anti-West campaign.[2]

The reader will recall that in 1958 the opposition to Metro concentrated on the part of the county outside the city. In 1962, however, the opposition, led by Mayor West, did an about-face and concentrated on the city. That is to say, they focused on the area of their own greatest strength rather than on the area of their opponents' presumed greatest weakness.[3] Their strength was derived, of course, from the city's political machine, and it was decided to operate that machine in much the same way that it usually operated.

Thus in May 1962 the Mayor called a series of secret meetings to oil the gears of his machine. City councilmen and employees were invited to participate, and it was decided to use policemen

1. It will be recalled that in 1958 the prime effort of the pro-Metro forces was to "explain the charter."

2. This description of the pro-Metro plan of attack is endorsed by numerous observers of the campaign, some of whom, indeed, were campaign activists as well. Interviews with Robert Horton, November 11, 1962; Amon Evans, Publisher, the Nashville *Tennessean*, November 26, 1962; Clifford Allen, County Tax Assessor, November 29, 1962; Edwin Hunt, Legal Counsel for the 1958 and 1962 Charter Commissions, December 14, 1962; James Roberson, December 18, 1962; and Joe Torrence, Finance Director, City of Nashville, November 29, 1962.

3. Both James H. Roberson and Mrs. J. D. Sanders, Women's Division Chairman of the CCBG, felt that the anti-Metro forces could have defeated Metro had they concentrated on the county. Interviews, December 18 and December 1, 1962.

and firemen and their wives to distribute anti-Metro literature.

Reliance was thus placed on the ability of city councilmen, policemen, firemen, and wives to gain access to the city's voters. It was realized of course that although such efforts had been successful in the past, the factor of some eighty thousand hostile annexed-area residents presented enormous new problems. But the Mayor was determined to work hard to bring about the defeat of the charter. So was the Nashville *Banner*.

CAMPAIGN ISSUES

The issues in the 1962 campaign are presented here under the headings, "Assault on the Status Quo" and "Defense of the Status Quo." In thus presenting the major issues it has not been possible to avoid dealing also with some of the activities undertaken by each side. For example, an important issue in the campaign concerned the anti-Metro activities of Nashville's policemen and firemen, thus making the activity itself an issue. The use of statements from the Nashville newspapers to illustrate major issues is another example of the difficulty in trying to separate issues from activities, for the statements also were activities either for or against Metro. Indeed, the papers actually bore a very heavy share of the day-to-day disputation.

Assault on the Status Quo.   The proponents of Metro sought to maximize dissatisfaction with the governmental status quo in Nashville and Davidson County. They attempted to present "things as they are" in as bad a light as possible.

Thus the proponents charged that Nashville's annexation of a large residential area was characteristic of the city administration and its methods. The *Tennessean* continually posed the alternatives: Metro or more annexation? They repeated over and over that more annexations were inevitable because the city would need more taxes to finance its heavy spending program and because this was the way Ben West operated.[4] Clearly this was meant to disturb county residents, particularly those adjacent to

4. The Nashville *Tennessean*, June 22, June 27, 1962.

the new city limits. Residents of Donelson and Madison were special targets in that both had voted against Metro in 1958.[5]

In a similar vein, the *Tennessean* sought to portray the annexed residents as exceedingly dissatisfied. It featured numerous articles quoting homeowners in these areas. One such article was entitled "Annex Woe Forcing Widow to Flee The City." "It's not that I want to live further out," said the widow, "but I'm so disgusted with the city and its government that I don't want to be where they can have anything to do with me!"[6]

Besides the annexation issue, Metro's proponents also played up the green-sticker episode. Thus most of the talks sponsored by such pro-Metro groups as the Citizens for Better Government and the League of Women Voters managed to work the green sticker into their agenda.

On the day of the charter referendum (June 28, 1962) the *Tennessean* carried an article characteristic of what the pro-Metro forces had been saying. One of the city councilmen supporting Metro was quoted as follows:

> The $10.00 has become a symbol of taxation without representation. . . . The people out in the county hate it . . . because it was levied by a legislative body in which they were not represented. . . . The green sticker has become a symbol of arbitrary power. . . .

The proponents of Metro also attempted to associate the opposition with as many undesirable, characteristically urban phenomena as possible. Local law enforcement, for example, had been an issue for some time. The Nashville police had upon occasion been embroiled in scandal, and now the *Tennessean* accelerated its denunciations of this situation. It sought to keep "the sad state of law enforcement" and "police corruption" continually before the reading public.[7] The Nashville police, along with the

5. Interviews with James Roberson, December 18, 1962 and Mrs. J. D. Sanders, Women's Division Citizens' Committee for Better Government, December 1, 1962. See also the Nashville *Tennessean,* June 14, June 24, June 27, 1962.

6. The Nashville *Tennessean,* June 18, 1962.

7. The Nashville *Tennessean,* May 31, June 15, June 17, June 22, June 23, 1962.

firemen, were also represented as the major instruments in Ben
West's campaign to block Metro.

Articles appeared telling of policemen passing out leaflets and
auto stickers against consolidated government.[8] One such article
stated:

> Working behind an avalanche of funds solicited from the anti-
> consolidation war chest, all 370 policemen—on and off duty—
> will be pressed into the drive. . . .
> The policemen will be joined by 425 city firemen and both
> groups—as usual—will be violating city civil service regulations
> which prevent civil service employees from engaging in political
> activity.

Still another important issue concerned the schools. As a pro-
Metro issue, emphasis was placed on the idea that consolidation
would eliminate the sort of intra-community bickering over
schools that resulted from Nashville's annexation policy.

Arguments about the duplication of offices and personnel also
figured prominently in the proponents' campaign to discredit the
existing state of things. The main thrust, of course, was that
consolidated government would save money by eliminating much
overlapping and duplication.

A few Metro supporters declared somewhat more carefully that
consolidation would bring more for the tax dollar and omitted
any reference to an absolute reduction in costs.

At one point the issue flared into a heated controversy. On
June 11, the Tennessee Taxpayers Association, a nonpartisan
businessman's organization, completed its report on the probable
fiscal consequences of the adoption of Metro. The report was then
released by the charter commission over the vigorous objections
of Joe Torrence. It estimated that Metro could result in an annual
savings of several hundred thousand dollars, perhaps even mil-
lions, although it made it clear that governmental costs would go
up under either system. It anticipated also that unless consolidated
government were adopted the county tax rate would increase

8. *Ibid.*, June 17, June 21, June 28, 1962.

sharply. This the opponents of Metro heatedly denied, and for a few days the battle, led by the two newspapers, raged.

Additional efforts to discredit the status quo included an attack on the county's private fire departments. The *Tennessean* carried a number of stories depicting the plight of "non-subscribers" under the existing system. One such story carried a picture of a man in Donelson looking dejectedly at the ruins of a storage building. The man was quoted as saying:

> "I called the fire department and they said they had formed some new rules. They said they weren't putting out anybody's house that wasn't a subscriber. . . . I offered to pay them a reasonable price to come out here and put out the fire. Instead they just came out here and stood around and watched it burn. I figured $250.00 would be a reasonable price."[9]

A few days earlier, the paper reported, another privately owned fire department had stood by and watched a service station go up in flames. "We wouldn't fight it because he wasn't a subscriber," explained Lorrence Allen, Chief of the Joywood Fire Department. "You pay, we serve, that's our motto."[10]

Defense of the Status Quo. Those who opposed the 1962 consolidation charter did not attempt to answer every attack made on the status quo. No real effort was made, for example, to refute the charge of police corruption, much of which, indeed, was beyond denial, nor to cover up the anti-Metro activities of city policemen and firemen. Nor was mention often made of the green sticker or the schools. On the other hand, the defenders of the status quo did come up with some charges of their own. Their allegations were not very different, however, from those that had been made in 1958. The real difference was that this time the city administration and its political apparatus were not answering the charges but instead stood check by jowl with those making them. In many of their statements, in fact, the city administration made amply clear that it regarded consolidation as a simultaneous

9. *Ibid.*, April 19, 1962.
10. *Ibid.*

attack upon the established City of Nashville, the existing (and energetic) administration, and the person of Ben West. For all these reasons, and many others, the opponents felt justified in activating their political machine, which, as everyone knew, depended upon the face-to-face contacts of the police and firemen.

Concerning the important annexation issue, the chief thrust of the anti-Metro forces was that is was *necessary*, and that despite difficulties the city was providing municipal services as rapidly as possible. They contended that annexation was necessary both for financial reasons and because the city had to grow. If it did not grow the city would eventually waste away, they argued.

The argument further ran that both annexation and consolidation involve serious limitations because of political problems, costly delays, and legal difficulties, but that constitutional obstacles might ensnarl consolidation for years. Thus although one could expect some difficulties from annexation these would not be as severe as those resulting from Metro. An effort was made to reinforce arguments of this sort by reference to Miami's metro shortcomings, in spite of the fact that Miami did not involve city-county consolidation, and in particular to the rash of litigation it produced.

The West administration also attempted, rather imaginatively, to mitigate the fear of annexation among suburban residents. On June 19 the city council adopted a resolution pledging no additional annexations until the residents of the newly annexed areas received the same municipal services as the residents of the old city. The *Banner* gave this resolution extensive publicity, but proponents of Metro charged that this was sheer trickery and could be made void at any time simply by another resolution.[11]

Another favorite argument of Metro's opponents was that the City of Nashville was a going concern already providing a great variety of municipal services. Two days before the referendum,

11. Perhaps this was not such a good idea from the standpoint of the anti-Metro forces, for it many well have helped publicize the annexation predictions of the pro-Metro forces.

for example, a *Banner* article declared that the City of Nashville provided 707 separate services. The *Banner* earlier had printed a cartoon representing the "city government" as a flourishing and productive apple tree about to be dug up by a shady looking character labeled "factional politics." Next to him stood a scrawny little shrub labeled "metro substitute."[12]

In a similar vein, Mayor West appeared on television a week before the vote and replied to his critics:

> We are called upon to decide by our votes whether we will continue with the known and tested structure of our present city and county governments—imperfect as they may be—or embark on an attempted "consolidation" of these two governments with a metropolitan charter which is novel, untried, untested, and the constitutionality of which is yet to be ascertained.
>
> Metro is presented as a cure-all for the ills of local government, a magic formula that will bring more services, yet cost less money —a Utopian system that would bring a new wave of unity and harmony to Nashville. You know human nature better than that. . . .[13]

West thus characteristically coupled his defense of the city government with the charge that Metro was an ocean upon which thoughtful men ought not to embark. They should not, he said, vote to abolish the city in favor of a lot of false claims.

West sought also to expose the attacks upon his person as an attempt to blind the voters to the real issues. Ben West, he suggested, was not a real issue.[14] "You don't," he said, "burn down the house just to get rid of one rat." He charged, in addition, that no mayor and no public official had ever been "subjected to the abuse, calculated slander, insult, and unsupported accusation to which this city's morning newspaper had subjected me over a number of years."

In addition, Metro's opponents saw a variety of dire consequences to follow from the adoption of the charter. Chief among

12. The Nashville *Banner,* June 18, 1962.
13. *Ibid.,* June 21, 1962.
14. *Ibid.*

these were control by a political faction led by the *Tennessean,*
centralization of power, and spot-zoning in behalf of liquor stores.

Opponents frequently charged that the proponents of Metro
were people who wanted to run Nashville, which they could not
do while Ben West resisted. West himself felt that the *Tennessean*
wanted to dictate to him and because they could not they were
determined to get rid of him.[15] The *Tennessean,* it was said,
wanted to enhance its stature as a "progressive" Southern newspaper which could win "liberal" battles.

In its designs the paper allegedly had the support of a number
of politicians who in June of 1962 were "on the outside." Exactly
who these people were varied with the bearer of the story; but
Briley, Clifford Allen, and such young attorneys as George Cate,
Jr., and Charles Warfield were frequently mentioned.

Fears and apprehensions regarding the undermining of states'
rights also figured prominently in the anti-Metro campaign, with
John Birchers leading the way. A typical statement of this attitude
appeared in a *Banner* letter to the editor printed on the day of the
referendum. The letter stated that "1313" in Chicago was seeking
to promote collectivism through the consolidation of governmental units.[16] "Under such a program it is apparent that political
state boundaries and state sovereignty would disappear."

"Mayor Ben West has confined liquor stores to the old city
area, but under the terms of the proposed Metro Charter whiskey
could be sold throughout the newly annexed territory and possibly
over the entire county." So declared a June 20 article in the
Banner. The contention was based on the fact that spot zoning
could occur under Metro and that the charter vested in the
General Services District certain powers and functions previously
exercised by the City of Nashville. As in 1958, this was an un-

15. See the Nashville *Banner,* June 21, June 25, 1962 and the Nashville
Tennessean, June 23, 1962. Interview with Ben West, Mayor, City of
Nashville, November 29, 1962.

16. The "1313" group is a collection of associations of officials and
governmental authorities whose headquarters are in Chicago. These associations (such as the Council of State Governments) are service agencies
and possess only the capacity to give advice and make studies.

welcome prospect to many of the area's churchgoers. In 1958, however, the *Banner* had indignantly refuted the allegation as impossible under the enabling act.

As for "overlapping and duplication" the chief thrust of the anti-Metro people was that tax increases were unavoidable with all the services the proponents were promising. Many of the charter's opponents suggested that the promises and claims for Metro would be hard to keep, especially the promise offered by the Tennessee Taxpayers Association.

Anti-Metro forces further charged that the proposed charter would not in fact end duplication, overlapping, and fragmentation. It would not, for example, dissolve the six "satellite cities" in Davidson County, although it did propose to abolish Nashville. Furthermore, the charter permitted the continued existence of various utility districts and, worse yet, provided for the creation of still more districts.[17]

In addition, the provisions of the charter governing the executive branch of the proposed metropolitan government were said to amount to "fragmented authority." A *Banner* editorial stated that the Metro mayor would not have full authority over financial matters because of the independently elected tax assessor, county trustee, and county court clerk. This was a favorite argument of Mayor West.

Opponents also alleged, of course, that Metro would be unconstitutional. The major grounds for challenging its constitutionality were that there had been an unconstitutional delegation of legislative power to the Metro charter commission; that Amendment eight to the Tennessee Constitution did not anticipate an entirely new entity such as a "metropolitan government"; and that the charter abridged the terms of constitutional officers. Numerous articles in the *Banner* underscored these challenges and emphasized the "cloud of legal doubt" hanging over the charter.[18] It was even suggested, with a letter from a New York bonding

17. The Nashville *Banner,* May 28, June 26, 1962.
18. *Ibid.,* May 17, May 28, June 19, 1962.

firm used in support, that so long as legal uncertainties remained, bonds issued by the new government would not be approved.[19]

INTEREST ALIGNMENTS AND ACTIVITIES

The following listings present the major interest groups and individuals[20] that were active for or against the 1962 charter. (For purposes of this study an "interest group" is an association of persons making demands upon other associations of persons, including both public and private bodies.)

Announced Official Position of Interest
Groups and Individuals

For the Charter   *Against the Charter*

INTEREST GROUPS

For the Charter	Against the Charter
Nashville Area Chamber of Commerce	Goodlettsville Area Chamber of Commerce
Education Council Incorporated	Members of Nashville Fire and Police Departments
Nashville Junior Chamber of Commerce	Nashville Building and Trades Council
League of Women Voters	Painters' Local 456
Federation of Business and Professional Women	Davidson County Democratic League
Five Jaycee and two Jaycette groups (chiefly suburban)	Officials of the small cities in Davidson County
Civic Committee on Public Education	

19. *Ibid.*, June 20, 1962.
20. Some of the persons named here were spokesmen for an interest group but were also conspicuous in the campaign as individuals. An effort was made to discuss individually only those group leaders who either appeared also as individuals or could not speak for their entire group.

The reason these particular persons are listed is that their names appeared most frequently in the newspapers and in the author's interviews of twenty-one "key observers" in the area. The key observers were selected arbitrarily but on the basis of previous research in Nashville by Daniel Elazar, David Grubbs, David Booth, and Jeanne Claire Ridley. Clearly, the procedure of asking reputedly key observers to name influential persons provides no rigorous proof that the persons named were actually most influential in the Metro campaign, and no such inference is intended. However, it is some indication of influence and opinion leadership.

For the Charter *Against the Charter*

INTEREST GROUPS (cont'd.)

For the Charter	Against the Charter
Citizens Committee for Better Government	Negro traditionalists[21]
Members of the Charter Commission	The Nashville *Banner*
Council of Jewish Women	
Davidson County Association of Fire and Police Departments	
Negro intellectuals[21]	
The Nashville *Tennessean*	
Tennessee Taxpayers Association	

INDIVIDUALS

For the Charter	Against the Charter
County Judge Briley	Mayor West
County Tax Assessor Allen	Thomas J. Anderson (John Birch leader)
County Trustee Robinson	
County Sheriff Jett	Albert Williams
Nashville Vice-Mayor Angela	Councilman Aubrey Gillem
Some labor leaders	Lewis Frazer
Some members of the Planning Commission staff	Councilman Gene Jacobs
Dan May	
George Cate, Jr.	

21. The terms "traditionalists" and "intellectuals" are used here solely for classificatory purposes and to illustrate the different approaches each group takes toward politics. No pejorative connotations are intended by the author. Thus the latter term is used simply because the group has a high percentage of university professors.

The "traditionalists" presumably view Negro political progress in much the same way that traditional ward politicians view progress—in terms of job-giving public projects in their districts. The newer "intellectuals," on the other hand, are supposed to have a much broader view of Negro progress. They think of expanding Negro political, educational, and employment opportunities in almost every sphere, and at least on a state-wide basis.

In considering below the role of interest groups and individuals, a distinction is made between "endorsements" and "campaigning." The latter refers to activities in addition to the act of endorsement. It is natural, of course, to focus major attention on groups engaging in actual campaign activities.

The Pro-Metro Campaigners: Groups.   As noted earlier, some of the major pro-Metro forces in Nashville and Davidson County decided to advance Metro by attacking the governmental status quo, or more directly by attacking Ben West and his city administration. Who specifically were the pro-Metro forces, and how did they seek to put over their strategy?

The determination to profit from the mistakes of 1958 was the impetus for the establishment of the Citizens' Committee For Better Government (CCBG). Led by James H. Roberson, a Nashville insurance man, the 1962 citizens' committee became a major weapon in the hands of the pro-Metro forces, for it undertook to provide the very block-by-block organization that had been so conspicuously absent in 1958.[22]

Roberson first applied his considerable talents in behalf of Metro just before the August 1960 Democratic primary. He and Silliman Evans, Jr., then publisher of the *Tennessean*, endeavored to get a slate of candidates for the General Assembly committed to Metro. Due in large measure to promises of support and threats of opposition by the *Tennessean*, the delegation agreed to promote another try at Metro.

After the private act creating a new charter commission emerged from the legislature, the Citizens' Committee for Better Government was formed.[23] Mrs. J. D. Sanders, then Secretary of

22. The bulk of the material in this section comes from the author's interviews with Roberson and Mrs. J. D. Sanders, head of the Women's Division, Citizens' Committee for Better Government.

23. Interviews with James Roberson, December 18, 1962, and Amon Evans, November 26, 1962. The lion's share of its financial support came from individual contributions, Silliman Evans, Jr., contributed some $2250.00. Large contributions also came from Garner Robinson, County Trustee ($500), Victor Johnson ($500) and Dan May ($250).

the Madison Chamber of Commerce, was approached and agreed to head a women's division.

The CCBG immediately set out to form a volunteer vote-canvassing organization. They intentionally shied away from "big names" and tried instead to fill their lists with salesmen, insurance agents, service station people, and above all with women from various walks of life.

On September 1, 1961, a meeting was called of the key women in the CCBG to maintain interest while the charter commission was deliberating. Members were urged to attend the public hearings of the charter group and to express their views. According to Roberson, the CCBG sought provisions in the charter that would help sell it, including a large council and the election, rather than appointment, of the court clerk, tax assessor, and trustee—all of whom were "proven vote-getters."[24]

By January 1962 a number of organizations had affiliated themselves with the CCBG. Among them were the League of Women Voters, the Council of Jewish Women, the Civic Committee on Public Education, the Education Council (a teachers' organization), and three Business and Professional Women's Clubs.

In April the CCBG persuaded George H. Cate, Jr., a young attorney and locally well known, to serve as general chairman. It also set up a speakers' bureau of some twenty-five persons, including charter commission members, several attorneys, and some women. Once again, however, "big names" were avoided.

Roberson and Mrs. Sanders meanwhile had been expanding the organization. In February a newsletter was sent to the eight hundred-odd individuals on their list urging a "thorough organization down to the precinct, street, and block level in order that we might reach every eligible voter in Davidson County." The various ward chairmen were urged to appoint councilmanic district chairmen, who were urged to appoint a precinct leader in

24. Interview with James Roberson, December 18, 1962.

each precinct, who in turn were to appoint street and block leaders. "If this procedure is followed in all areas of the county," the newsletter declared in bold letters, "we shall have no trouble in contacting each and every voter."

By May the CCBG itself had a hard core of some fifteen hundred canvassers, and with its affiliated organizations the pro-Metro forces could count on upwards of five thousand workers. All 108 precincts were in some measure organized with volunteer canvassers.[25]

The vast majority of the canvassers were women, moreover, and had no compunction about knocking on doors and making phone calls.[26] Roberson, in fact, attributes much of Metro's success to the women. "The housewives did the job," he said, "walking up and down with their fact-sheets."[27]

The "fact-sheets" carried around by the canvassers were rough-hewn folders containing fourteen mimeographed pages describing and praising the Metro charter and criticizing the governmental status quo.

Besides canvassing activities, the CCBG, in co-operation with its affiliated organizations, sponsored some 250 neighborhood meetings—the majority of them in higher-income areas—circulated handbills,[28] sent out mailings, and sponsored newspaper ads.

Enough has been said already to indicate the part of the *Tennessean* in the Metro campaign. Long a foe of Ben West, the *Tennessean* carried on a lion's share of the day-to-day disputation. Its pages fairly dripped with the issues, whether "genuine" or "fabricated." In addition, the *Tennessean*, or perhaps its publisher acting as an individual, helped to formulate the pro-Metro strategy and contributed a very large sum to the CCBG.

25. On June 3, 1963, the *Tennessean* published a list of the CCBG ward and district leaders. Every city ward and county district had its canvass leader, and every one was a woman.

26. Interviews with Robert Horton, November 11, 1962, James Roberson, December 18, 1962, and Mrs. J. D. Sanders, December 1, 1962.

27. Interview with James Roberson, December 18, 1962.

28. *Ibid.*

Mayor West told this author that the *Tennessean* actually set up the CCBG. It is quite true, of course, that James H. Roberson worked closely with the *Tennessean*'s publisher, Silliman Evans, Jr., and it is also true that the largest financial contribution to the CCBG came from Evans (some $2,250 according to Roberson). But the *Tennessean*'s treasurer told this author that it was Mr. Evans's personal contribution. Roberson, however, referred to it as the *Tennessean*'s contribution.

However that may be, the *Tennessean* and its publisher were important assets to the pro-Metro forces.

Metro had been a special project for the Nashville Area League of Women Voters ever since the 1958 referendum and was generally supported by League members as a desirable reform.

Some twenty members of the League participated in the sort of canvassing activities advocated by the CCBG. In addition, the League sponsored workshops and held neighborhood coffees in behalf of metropolitan government. Each member was asked to give a coffee in her home, with speakers sponsored by the League. Mrs. Gus Kuhn, President of the League at the time of the vote, estimated that hundreds of coffee hours were held. She singled out for special credit in this regard attorney George Barrett and Nashville City Councilman Scott Fillebrown.

The day before the vote the League provided information booths at all shopping centers and passed out pamphlets, handbills, and auto stickers.

The Civic Committee on Public Education, a nonteachers' organization, and the Education Council, a teacher's organization, constituted the "education group" in the 1962 campaign, and both strongly supported metropolitan government.

According to Dr. James Phythyon, a physician and the Civic Committee representative with the CCBG, his organization had been set up expressly to promote metropolitan government and to emphasize the educational aspect of it.[29] Its membership in-

29. Interview with Dr. James Phythyon, Chairman of Projects Committee Civic Committee on Public Education, November 28, 1962.

cluded George Cate, Jr., several prominent doctors' wives, elements from various PTA groups, and individuals from the League of Women Voters.

Both the Civic Committee and the Education Council became affiliated with the CCBG and provided volunteer canvassers. The former also sponsored a series of public meetings at which charter commission members spoke.[30]

The Education Council, led by Robert Bogen, worked closely with both the CCBG and the Civic Committee. As a teachers' organization the Council favored an elected school board, and during the deliberations of the charter commission it sponsored seminars to promote this preference at some thirty schools.

As noted earlier, the charter commission unanimously endorsed the charter filed on April 6, 1962. During the campaign, moreover, the commission members individually and collectively engaged in a number of pro-Metro activities.

Individually many charter commission members actively supported the charter. Among them were Carmack Cochran, Victor Johnson, Cecil Branstetter, Harlan Dodson, and Alexander Looby. Many charter body members also answered questions submitted to the *Tennessean*'s question-and-answer column.

On June 26, two days before the vote, the entire commission (except Mr. Torrence) appeared on television to answer questions and praise consolidated government.

The Council of Jewish Women, with Mrs. Gilbert Fox as President, was also affiliated with the CCBG and supplied many vote-canvassers. Like the "education group," the Council of Jewish Women was especially concerned about the school issue.

A number of prominent Negro leaders endorsed Metro and spoke in its behalf. Among them were Fisk University Professor Vivian Henderson, several doctors at Meharry Medical College, Miss Lurelia Freeman of the Language Department at Tennessee A & I, attorney Avon Williams, and NAACP President Mrs.

---

30. *Ibid.* Few were held, however, in the lower-income sections. East, North, and South Nashville were not covered.

C. M. Hayes. Dean of the group was attorney Z. Alexander Looby, a venerable and much respected Negro leader who reputedly carried a great deal of influence with his people.

Professor Henderson was probably the most active of this group. In addition to his television appearance, he spoke to a number of gatherings sponsored by the CCBG and affiliated organizations. His theme—indeed the theme of most of this group—was that Metro was really a question of good government versus antiquated government. Metro, he felt, was in the interest of a better community, without whose growth all would suffer.[31] Considerations of this sort, many argued, took precedence over the fact that consolidation would dilute the voting power of the Negro community.

Pro-Metro Campaigners: Individuals. The individuals who campaigned in behalf of metropolitan government—Judge Briley, Tax Assessor Allen, hosiery mill executive Dan May, and attorney George H. Cate, Jr.—have been introduced in other contexts. Cate, for example, was Chairman of the CCBG and as such made numerous talks before neighborhood or community gatherings. A very able speaker with a respected academic background at Vanderbilt University, Cate made a good impression almost everywhere, and he appeared often in the columns of the *Tennessean.*

Dan May, owner of the May Hosiery Mills, made frequent public appearances and contributed a substantial sum of money to CCBG. He too was an able speaker—and witty as well.

Briley and Allen also made frequent and important appearances in behalf of Metro. Allen, however, was not able to stir up much support for his efforts from the Citizens Committee, chiefly because of strong doubts about the popularity of his public image.[32] But Allen was nevertheless a proven vote-getter. He had been a state senator and candidate for governor and was

31. Interview with Dr. Vivian Henderson, Professor of Economics, Fisk University, December 17, 1962.
32. Interview with James Roberson, December 18, 1962.

a dynamic public speaker besides. Consequently, Glenn Bainbridge, a wealthy Nashville realtor, paid for a number of Clifford Allen's television appearances.

A further source of important and strategic individual support came from some members of the staff of the City-County Planning Commission. Their contribution was not in the form of campaigning but in supplying on request technical and strategic advice growing out of their impressions of the 1958 campaign, especially to Judge Briley and the CCBG. Director of the Research Division, Robert Horton, and his assistants, Joe Haas and Robert Puryear, supplied requested data and generally made available to Metro supporters their expert advice.

Pro-Metro Endorsements. In 1958 and again in 1962 the Nashville Chamber of Commerce endorsed Metro. In 1962, however, there was substantial opposition within the Chamber. The actual vote of the Board of Governors was 14 to 8 and was taken by secret ballot because of the rather intimidating presence of both Mayor West and Judge Briley.

In May the Nashville Junior Chamber of Commerce endorsed Metro on grounds that it would eliminate duplication, assure properly apportioned councilmanic districts, and prevent unwise annexation.

The Nashville Federation of Business and Professional Women as an organization endorsed Metro and affiliated with the Citizens Committee. As individuals, the membership provided a number of canvassers for the latter group.

The Donelson, Uptown, Westown, Woodbine, and Old Hickory Jaycees endorsed Metro. The Nashville and Old Hickory Jaycettes also endorsed Metro.

In 1958 the so-called private firemen and policemen supplied much of the legwork for the opposition to Metro; in 1962, they formally endorsed the charter. Their change of heart was apparently due to the fact that fire protection was an "urban" service under the charter, thus enabling private fire departments to continue operating. At a meeting on June 2, the group was apprised of this fact by a county magistrate.

Mention has already been made of the endorsement by the Tennessee Taxpayers Association and the financial report it furnished to the Charter Commission. Donald Jackson, the Association's President, publicly committed himself to Metro and defended the Taxpayers Association's financial report when it came under fire from anti-Metro forces.

During the campaign Sheriff Jett, Trustee Robinson, and Vice-Mayor Anglea all publicly endorsed Metro. All had proved themselves substantial vote-getters and were thus regarded by the pro-Metro people as desirable allies.

Although "labor" as such neither supported nor opposed Metro,[33] some labor leaders announced their personal support. Chief among them was Matthew Lynch, Secretary of the Tennessee State Labor Council. Four days before the vote Lynch appeared on television with five others and predicted that metropolitan government would accelerate industrial development by providing good government and thus result in additional jobs. Glenn Cornwell, President of Ford Local 737, the largest local union in the state, appeared on the same program in support of Metro.

According to Lynch, laboring men and women provided a number of volunteer canvassers and phone solicitors for the CCBG and affiliated organizations.[34] Many, he added, were won over to Metro by the charter's provision for a large council and by the efficiency argument.

Anti-Metro Campaigners: Groups. During the first week of June the Goodlettsville Area Chamber of Commerce met and passed a resolution condemning the 1962 charter. According to its President, Dr. Donald R. Dunning, a dentist, the people in Goodlettsville were satisfied with things as they were and did not feel safe in entrusting their future to a metropolitan-wide council. Many felt, moreover, than none of the benefits from Metro would affect them, at least not for a long time.

33. Interview with James Roberson, December 18, 1962.
34. Interview with Matthew Lynch, Secretary, Tennessee State Labor Council, December 18, 1962.

Dr. Dunning attempted to counteract the fear of annexation by seeking a legal opinion as to whether the City of Nashville could in fact annex Goodlettsville. A prominent Nashville attorney advised the Chamber that in his opinion the Goodlettsville municipal corporation could not be annexed "now or in the future,"[35] whereupon the Goodlettsville *Gazette* noted that pro-Metro forces had been trying to scare voters in the smaller incorporated towns into believing that towns incorporated after March 1, 1955, could be annexed.[36]

On June 12 twenty-four government officials from Nashville, Davidson County, and the smaller suburban cities met in Goodlettsville to map their campaign strategy. The meeting was sponsored by the Goodlettsville Chamber of Commerce, and a promotional effort, using various mailings, was approved.

Nashville firemen and policemen formed the main cogs in the West political machine and its 1962 campaign against Metro.

Enough has been said to indicate the role of the *Banner*, long a loyal supporter of Ben West.

Most of the officials of the smaller cities had opposed Metro in 1958.

On June 21 the *Banner* carried a series of the statements from the Boards of Commissioners of Belle Meade, Berry Hill, Oak Hill, Forest Hills, and Goodlettsville. The statements declared that the smaller cities refused to give up their charters. This group of officials also paid for a full-page "no-Metro" ad on June 26.[37]

Considerable emphasis has already been placed on the fact that large numbers of "traditionalist" Negroes, led by City

35. The Nashville *Banner*, June 8, 1962.

36. This date was the effective date of the general annexation law mentioned above. The law did not specifically exempt from annexation places incorporated *after* March 8, 1955, although it did recognize the integrity of then existing municipal corporations. There has been no litigation on this point to date.

37. Interview with Dr. James Dunning, President Goodlettsville Area Chamber of Commerce, November 30, 1962.

Councilman Robert Lillard, looked upon Metro as a dilution of their voting strength.

Lillard utilized his own organization to combat Metro and to stress this undesirable feature. According to Lillard himself, his organization sent out in his district some three thousand mimeographed leaflets stressing the loss of Negro voting strength under Metro. Similar leaflets were distributed in other districts by Negro Boy Scouts under the direction of the Davidson County Democratic League.[38]

In addition Lillard made frequent personal appearances, often to debate Metro proponents. At such debates he commonly stressed Metro's "centralization" and legal uncertainties.

Anti-Metro Campaigners: Individuals. Mayor West's activities in opposition to Metro have been discussed above.

South Nashville City Councilman Gene "Little Evil" Jacobs has doubtless precipitated as much political controversy as any single person in recent times in Nashville.[39] About a month before the Metro vote, Jacobs announced that he was going to fight Metro "harder than anyone," whereupon he plastered his house and his car (and the cars of one or two of his helpers) with "no-Metro" stickers, got his picture in the paper with a blind friend carrying a radio also plastered with no-Metro stickers, and spread around some signs proclaiming that "Russia Has One Government" and "Castro has Metro."

Jacobs managed to arouse a strong protest from the *Tennessean* when he subsequently announced his reason for opposition to Metro—that it would raise the rents in all the houses in South Nashville.

Thomas J. Anderson, a John Birch Society leader and a local publisher, quickly voiced his opposition to Metro. On June 2 he said on WLAC Radio that Metro "plays into the hands of the

38. The use of the Boy Scouts raised a minor storm from the *Tennessean*. See June 18, 1962, issue.

39. Jacobs has served jail terms, and in 1963 he was convicted of conspiracy in tampering with absentee ballots in a general election.

socialists" and that it "would be another nail driven into the coffin of states' rights." Anderson also let it be known to this author that the socialists were trying to "metro-ize the county" and that was why he was against it.[40] Several hundred auto bumper stickers distributed by Anderson proclaimed "Kill Metro Before it Multiplies: Big Government Means Small People."

Anti-Metro Endorsements.   Just before the June 28 vote the Nashville Building and Trades Council and Painters Union Local 456 announced their opposition to Metro. The former expressed itself by majority vote of the executive council, the latter in a regular meeting attended by some two hundred members.[41]

The Davidson County Democratic League was a newly formed Negro organization set up to promote Negro voter registration. On June 26 the DCDL announced that it would oppose consolidated government, and it subsequently aided in the distribution of anti-Metro literature.[42]

Anti-Metro Individuals.   City Councilman Aubrey Gillem, a long-time West supporter and champion of annexation, early made known his opposition to Metro.

"Judge" Albert Williams (an honorary title at the time of the vote) had opposed Metro in 1958 and still opposed it in 1962. As a lawyer, his comments on the charter were occasionally solicited and printed by the *Banner*.[43]

Lewis Frazer, a prominent citizen of Forest Hills, was also a two-time opponent of Metro. An "ultra-conservative," Frazer held views on the subject similar to those of Thomas J. Anderson.

CONCLUSIONS

As noted in Chapter Four, the following groups have been listed in the literature as predominantly favoring reorganization: metropolitan newspapers; Leagues of Women Voters; central city chambers of commerce; central city officials; academic

40. Interview with Thomas J. Anderson, November 29, 1962.
41. The Nashville *Banner*, June 27, 1962.
42. The Nashville *Tennessean*, June 18, 1962.
43. See the Nashville *Banner*, June 27, 1962.

groups or spokesmen; central city commercial or real estate interests.

In Nashville in 1962 one metropolitan newspaper, the *Tennessean*, supported Metro and the other, the *Banner*, opposed. In 1958, however, both newspapers supported Metro. The Nashville experience therefore supports the proposition that metropolitan newspapers tend to support reorganization. In four chances in Nashville they supported reorganization three times.

Both the League of Women Voters and the Nashville Area Chamber of Commerce officially supported Metro. Thus the Nashville experience supports the proposition that these two groups tend to favor reorganization.

No data were gathered systematically on the position of central city officials *as a group*.[44] However, the Mayor and the Nashville firemen and policemen (including major officers) publicly opposed Metro. Many observers, including this writer, believe that the vast majority of city officials went along with the Mayor in opposition.[45]

The Nashville experience therefore does not support the hypothesis or, more accurately, it represents one datum in opposition to the hypothesis that central city officials tend to favor governmental reorganization in metropolitan areas.

No really conclusive data were uncovered on the position of academic spokesmen as a group. It was, however, a matter of public knowledge that Fisk University Professor Henderson, Vanderbilt Professor Grant, and Tennessee A & I Professor Lurelia Freeman endorsed Metro. This writer can state from his own experience that a number of professors at Vanderbilt both favored and voted for Metro. No claims are made, however, about the extent to which the professors who expressed their views to

44. One would have to know what a majority of the city officials did in order to generalize about them *as a group*. Even then, the size of the majority one way or the other would greatly qualify such generalizations.
45. Interviews with Robert Horton, November 11, 1962; Edwin Hunt, December 14, 1962; A. D. Gillem, Nashville City Councilman, December 22, 1962; Dick Battle, December 13, 1962; and Clifford Allen, County Tax Assessor, November 29, 1962.

this author were representative of the Vanderbilt faculty as a whole.

If the local PTAs and the Nashville Education Council are included in this category, moreover, further support is lent to the proposition. Thus the Nashville experience at least does not refute this proposition.

Although no really conclusive data were uncovered on the position of the area's commercial and real estate interests, the Nashville experience lends some support to the proposition that these interests tend to favor metropolitan reorganizations. Thus the Nashville Area Chamber of Commerce, several junior chambers of commerce, and the Tennessee Taxpayers Association publicly endorsed Metro. It seems likely that the majority of commercial and real estate interests were represented by these organizations and approved of their position. One of the largest real estate owners in the city, moreover, financed Clifford Allen's television appearances on behalf of Metro.[46]

Anti-Metro Groups. The proposition to be examined here in light of the Nashville experience is that the following groups tend to oppose governmental reorganizations in metropolitan areas: farmers and rural homeowners; county government officials; employees of fringe local governments.

As shown in the section below, the voters in the twenty county precincts classified as rural voted against Metro by 66 per cent. The Nashville experience therefore supports the proposition that farmers and rural homeowners tend to oppose governmental reorganization in metropolitan areas, at least when such reorganizations can be interpreted as the city "reaching out to get" rural areas.

No really conclusive data were uncovered on the position of county government employees as a group. It seems plausible, however, that the support of the County Judge (Briley), the County Tax Assessor (Allen), the County Trustee (Garner

46. Interview with James Roberson, Co-ordinator, Citizens' Committee for Better Government, December 18, 1962.

Robinson), and the County Sheriff (Leslie Jett) carried into the pro-Metro camp a great many county employees. Therefore the Nashville experience is probably at variance with the hypothesis that county government employees tend to oppose governmental reorganizations in metropolitan areas.

Due in part to the bitter opposition of the city administration, a great many people probably looked upon Metro as the county taking over the city. In other metropolitan areas the reverse interpretation has often been placed on a proposed governmental reorganization.

Enough evidence was uncovered on the position of fringe government employees as a group to conclude with some confidence that the Nashville experience supports the proposition that this group tends to oppose metropolitan reorganizations. The reader will recall that the Boards of Commissioners of Belle Meade, Berry Hill, Oak Hill, Forest Hills, and Goodlettsville publicly opposed Metro. It is quite plausible, moreover, that the officials and employees of such fringe governments would view area-wide government as a threat.

Thus the alignment of interest groups in Nashville's metropolitan integration process was generally consistent with similar integration processes elsewhere—with one very important exception. Neither central city officials nor county officials behaved in a manner consistent with the literature. In the opinion of the present author, the reason for this reversal is to be sought, simply, in the area's recent political history. In the period between referenda Mayor West and his allies committed themselves to the annexation effort, partly because Metro seemed unlikely to be resurrected—and even less likely to succeed if it were resurrected—and partly because the Mayor appeared to have become unpopular in the county in any event. Many county officials, at the same time, were angered by the green-sticker tax, by the annexation of county territory, and by what they regarded as the generally unseemly behavior of West's administration. Under these circumstances, a new try at Metro—which many of the area's citizens favored as a desirable reform in any case—loomed as a natural anticity, anti-West move. Judge Briley's own support was apparently motivated both by a belief in the desirability of consolidation and by a realization that he stood to emerge on top if the anti-West Metro move succeeded. The actual outcome, of course, proved that such thinking was far from implausible.

It is interesting to note, in addition, that Nashville's Metro succeeded despite the opposition of the central city's mayor. Some political scientists have argued that the support, or acquiescence, of this key figure is absolutely essential if a reorganization proposal is to succeed. Edward C. Banfield and Morton Grodzins, for example, have stated flatly that "where the central-city mayor opposes reorganization it will fail."[47]

It is also important to note carefully the make-up of the proponents of change in Nashville. One political scientist, writing immediately after the 1962 vote, suggested that the second Nashville campaign was "as if the professionals and the politicians had taken over from the amateurs and the do-gooders."[48] There is, of course, an important sense in which this is true, but some qualifications are necessary. It is quite true, for example, that under the experienced direction of James H. Roberson the pro-Metro forces—consisting mostly of civic associations—were formed into an effective vote-canvassing organization. It is also true that the two political titans of the area took opposite sides and had vital political stakes in the outcome.

In short, it is true that both the proponents and the opponents were better organized than in 1958, the former under the Citizens' Committee for Better Government—and Judge Briley—and the latter under Ben West's city machine.

On the other hand, the CCBG was little more than a loose coalition of heterogeneous elements held together by a common

---

47. *Government and Housing in Metropolitan Areas* (New York: McGraw Hill, 1958), p. 155.

48. David Booth, *Metropolitics: The Nashville Consolidation* (East Lansing, Michigan: Institute for Community Development and Services, Michigan State University, 1963), p. 85.

interest in a good government project. Thus Robert Horton, Research Director of the City-County Planning Commission, told this author that the group just managed to hang together through the day of the referendum and that they probably could not have stayed together on any issue but Metro.[49] The CCBG also relied on much the same sort of amateurs and do-gooders that the pro-Metro forces had relied upon in 1958, and that have been relied upon elsewhere. The only difference—and it was a very important difference—was the manner in which these groups were used.

It would appear, therefore, that the role of the civic associations in Nashville was that of an instrumentality for getting the job done. Edward Banfield has suggested that civic associations can be very useful for such purposes—when the problem is clear-cut and when the solution is well understood.[50] The problem in Nashville was apparently West and annexation, and the solution was Metro.

Whether the CCBG and Roberson were actually fronts for some "elite," or whether an elite failed to act because it was satisfied with what was happening, cannot be answered conclusively here. But it is doubtful that either was the case.

One could argue, of course, that the *Tennessean* was the real power behind the Metro effort, since it used its influence to get Metro revived, since it was perhaps instrumental in setting up the CCBG, and since it bore a heavy load in the actual campaign. It would seem plausible, moreover, that, given the existence of such ready-made issues as annexation and a crudely imposed wheel tax, a metropolitan newspaper might well put over a major governmental reorganization. But this argument is based on the existence of certain favorable conditions—on rather unique conditions, in this case. After all, the *Tennessean*'s position lost in 1958, despite the support of an impressive array of the area's business elite and of the other metropolitan newspaper as well.

49. Horton was very close to the campaign. Interview with Robert Horton, November 11, 1962.
50. Edward C. Banfield, *Political Influence* (New York: The Free Press, 1961), p. 297.

Perhaps conditions then were less favorable. Elitists might reply, of course, that the *Tennessean* learned its lesson in 1958 and thus set up an effective vote-canvassing organization in 1962.

This author, however, feels that the best efforts of the pro-Metro forces would have been futile in the absence of annexation and the green-sticker episode.

9

VOTER OPPOSITION AND SUPPORT

T HE central question of this study relates to opposition and support for governmental reorganization in metropolitan areas. In this chapter the interview and aggregate voting data from Nashville (1962) are examined to help understand such opposition and support.

VOTER ATTITUDE HYPOTHESES

In Chapter One, four hypotheses were gleaned from the relevant literature and offered as hypotheses to be tested in Nashville. In the present section the interview data collected in Nashville are brought to bear on these hypotheses. Only the data from the interviews[1] are considered.

1. "Don't know" and "no answer" responses are discarded in all cases and, for purposes of this study, null hypotheses are rejected when the probability value for chi square is lower than .05. For all frequency distributions with one degree of freedom corrections are made for continuity in computing chi squares.

The chi square test indicates the degree to which an observed frequency distribution differs from a random assortment. Thus a "p" of $< .05$ means that the probability of that frequency distribution occurring by chance is less than 1 in 20.

Strictly speaking, chi square "tests" a *null hypothesis*—that there is no significant difference between the observed distribution and what one would expect by chance. If this null hypothesis can be rejected, a probability statement can be made about the implied "alternative" hypothesis—that there *is* a significant difference.

Failure to reject a null hypothesis, however, does not necessarily establish its truth but only that the sample data offer no evidence against the hypothesis in terms of the standard agreed upon.

Before considering the actual hypotheses, however, a warning is in order. The reader should understand that the present research was done *after* the 1962 Metro vote. Consequently, in addition to any sampling error that might be present, the *ex post facto* nature of the research was likely to introduce a bias in favor of the actual outcome of the referendum—in this case on the pro-Metro side. Such discrepancies are common in *ex post facto* research.[2]

Dissatisfaction with Public Services under a Fragmented Structure. As stated above, the hypothesis to be tested here is that voters who are dissatisfied with their services are more likely to support reorganization than those who are satisfied.

Each respondent was first asked his opinion about local services. The question was deliberately left open-ended in order to provide a measure of the saliency of this issue among those interviewed. The question was: "On the whole, do you feel your local services are adequate or inadequate at the present time?" Fifty-four per cent of the 166 persons answering this question felt that their services were "inadequate." This would seem to indicate that there was considerable dissatisfaction with services in the Nashville area. The reader will recall that neither in Flint nor in Dayton was there such a high proportion of respondents dissatisfied with their services. In St. Louis, however, approximately 80 per cent of those interviewed indicated some dissatisfaction with services, although there was little consensus as to changes desired.

The higher proportion of dissatisfied respondents in Nashville and St. Louis was possibly a result of the protracted conflict about local government in each city before the research done there.

2. Herbert Hyman, *Survey Design and Analysis* (Glencoe, Illinois: The Free Press, 1955), p. 151. See also F. Mosteller et al., *The Pre-Election Polls of 1948* (New York: Social Science Research Council Bulletin #6, 1949), p. 213.

In the present study it is a good guess that such a bias occurred, for the actual county-wide vote for Metro was 57 per cent, whereas the sample percentage was 67 per cent. This subject is taken up below in more detail.

The ninety Nashville-area respondents who expressed general dissatisfaction with their services were next asked to select from a list of eight services the two that they felt were "most in need of improvement." These results are presented in Table IV.

TABLE IV

Services Named as "Most In Need Of Improvement" by Persons
Expressing General Dissatisfaction with Local Services
in Nashville and Davidson County, 1962

	Per cent	Number
Sewage disposal	25.9	42
Street and road maintenance	20.9	34
Police protection	14.8	24
Fire protection	10.5	17
Public schools	6.8	11
Parks and recreation	6.8	11
Water supply	6.8	11
Garbage collection	6.2	10
Number answering question		160[a]

a. Each respondent was asked to pick two services. Some picked only one.

Of course none of these data shows anything about support and opposition. Consequently, the respondents' answers to a question on how they voted were compared with the question: "On the whole, do you think your services are adequate or inadequate at the present time?" The results are shown in Table V.

TABLE V

Relationship between Dissatisfaction with Services
and Support for Reorganization

	Per cent	
	Answering	Answering
Vote	Adequate	Not Adequate
For reorganization	52.6	81.1
Against reorganization	47.4	18.9
N(=100%)	76	90
$X^2 = 14.09$, df $= 1$, $p < .001$		

These data indicate much greater support for reorganization among those not satisfied with services than among those satisfied; the data thus confirm the hypothesis as stated. It is worth emphasizing, however, that even among those expressing satisfaction more than half, 52.6 per cent, voted for the reorganization proposal.

Anticipation of Higher Taxes with Reorganization. The hypothesis tested here is that voters who anticipate higher taxes with reorganization are more likely to oppose it than those who do not anticipate higher taxes.

To discover something of the saliency of this issue compared with others, all respondents were first asked to state the most important reason causing them to vote either for or against the reorganization proposal.[3] Among those voting against the proposal, 23.7 per cent said that their decision was based on the belief that consolidation would cost them more in taxes. Although this percentage is not large (76.3 per cent expressed other reasons), it was the modal reason. The second most frequently cited reason, that the respondent himself would not have gotten anything from the consolidation, received 15.3 per cent of the responses. The difference between 23.7 per cent and 15.3 is of course not great, but this is one indication of the saliency of this issue.

Another indication of saliency, although a less direct one, can perhaps be seen in the responses to the same question by those who voted *for* consolidation. In this group 38.7 per cent indicated a belief that consolidation would result in greater efficiency and/ or lower cost. The next most frequently cited reason (to receive better services) received only 17.6 per cent of the responses.[4] The difference between 38.7 per cent and 17.6 per cent is of course greater than the above difference.

No important conclusions about the relationship between

3. See the last section in this chapter for a complete breakdown of the responses to this question.
4. See the last section in this chapter for a complete breakdown of the responses to this question.

anticipating higher taxes and opposition to reorganization can be drawn from these figures, nor was this approach designed to answer questions about this relationship. The next question was so designed, however.

Every respondent was asked a fixed-alternative question relating to taxes under consolidated government, should it pass. They were asked to say what they thought would happen to taxes "as a result of Metro." Would taxes be higher than they would have been without Metro, lower than they would have been without Metro, or the same as they would have been without Metro? It was assumed that the first response would indicate the extent to which people anticipated higher taxes with reorganization and the second and third would indicate the extent to which people did not anticipate higher taxes with reorganization.

In Table VI these responses are compared with those obtained from the question on how the respondents voted.

TABLE VI

Relationship between Anticipation of Higher Taxes with
Reorganization and Opposition to Reorganization

| | Per cent | |
| | Anticipating | Not anticipating |
Vote	higher taxes	higher taxes
For reorganization	41.4	85.7
Against reorganization	58.6	14.3
N(=100%)	70	98
$X^2 = 34.38$, df $= 1$, p $< .001$		

It is clear from Table VI that a majority of those who indicated that they anticipated higher taxes with reorganization voted against reorganization, whereas those who did not anticipate higher taxes voted overwhelmingly for reorganization. The sample data therefore support the hypothesis that voters who anticipate higher taxes with reorganization are more likely to oppose it than those who do not anticipate higher taxes.

The author also considered the possibility that this correlation represents as much the satisfaction or dissatisfaction with services variable as the anticipation or nonanticipation of higher taxes. If this were true, those persons not anticipating higher taxes ("yes" voters) would be predominantly the same persons as those currently dissatisfied with their services (also "yes" voters). Conversely, those persons anticipating higher taxes ("no" voters) would be predominantly the same persons as those currently satisfied with their services. This would suggest in turn that opposition to metropolitan reorganization can be explained equally well with either factor.

The data in Table VII lend some support to the author's hunch that opposition to reorganization can be explained equally well with either independent variable. Thus 92.7 per cent of those both dissatisfied with their services and *not* anticipating higher taxes were yes voters, whereas only 26.3 per cent of those both satisfied with their services and anticipating higher taxes were yes voters. More than 7 out of 10 in the latter group were *no* voters.[5]

It appears on the other hand that the anticipation of higher taxes variable is still relevant when the satisfaction with services variable is held constant, because among all voters dissatisfied with their services a much higher percentage of those not anticipating higher taxes (NAT) were for reorganization than those anticipating higher taxes (AT). Furthermore, among all satisfied voters also a much higher percentage of NATs were for reorganization than of ATs. Thus given the wording of the hypothesis being considered—that voters who anticipate higher taxes with reorganization are more likely to oppose than voters who do not anticipate higher taxes—these data do not require rejection of the hypothesis.

It is quite possible, of course, that most of the voters who were dissatisfied with their services in the Nashville area were simply unwilling, or unable, to believe that reorganization would bring

5. In addition, the chi square value for tach distribution, taken separately, is significant in terms of the agreed upon standard.

TABLE VII

Relationship of Satisfaction with Services
to Anticipation of Higher Taxes

	Per cent					
	Satisfied with services			Dissatisfied with services		
	Antici- pating higher taxes	Not antici- pating higher taxes	TOTAL	Antici- pating higher taxes	Not antici- pating higher taxes	TOTAL
For reorganization	26.3	87.5	52.6	63.3	92.7	81.1
Against reorganization	73.7	12.5	47.4	36.7	7.3	18.9
N(=100%)	38	32	76	30	55	90
	$X^2 = 24.797$, df $= 1$, p $< .001$			$X^2 = 9.607$, df $= 1$, p $< .01$		

higher taxes, even though they simultaneously believed that it *would* bring more services. In any case, the data from Nashville do suggest that more research is needed into the relationship between these two variables and opposition to metropolitan reorganization.

County "Suspicion" of the Central City and Its Government. The hypothesis tested here is that county voters who are "suspicious" of the central city are more likely to oppose reorganization than those who are not "suspicious" of the central city.[6]

The following questions were asked all respondents outside the City of Nashville. (Respondents in the recently annexed areas were not asked these questions.) They were asked to indicate whether they agreed or disagreed with the following statements printed on a card:

(1) This community (or area) is really a separate community (or area) from Nashville and should have a separate government.

(2) On the whole, big city politics are more corrupt than smaller city politics.

(3) As a rule, it is better to live in small communities with small governments than large communities with large governments.

Responses of agreement were regarded as indicating some measure of "suspicion." These data were then compared with those from the question on how respondents voted. The results, which are quite similar, are presented in Tables VIII, VIII-A and VIII-B.

If these three measures of suspicion are valid, there is a clear pattern of opposition to reorganization among those fringe-area voters who expressed suspicion of the central city. There is also a clear pattern of support among fringe-area voters who did not

---

6. An obvious way to bring data to bear on this question is a thorough analysis of the aggregate voting figures. However, in this section we are considering the attitudes of individual voters. The voting analysis is presented below.

express such suspicion. The sample data therefore support the hypothesis that outside voters who are suspicious of the central city are more likely to oppose reorganization than those who are not suspicious. The data are dependent, however, on the validity of the measures of "suspicion."

· One additional point is worthy of note. "Suspicious" voters, as indicated by the first question above, opposed reorganization proportionately more than "suspicious" voters, as indicated by the next two questions. There were only eighteen suspicious respondents to the first question, however; whereas there were more than thirty to the following questions. This author suspects

TABLE VIII

Relationship between Suspicion[a] of the Central City among Voters outside the City and Opposition to Reorganization

Vote	Per cent	
	Suspicious	Not suspicious
For reorganization	16.7	72.7
Against reorganization	83.3	27.3
N(=100%)	18	55
$X^2 = 15.37$, df $= 1$, p $< .001$		

a. As measured by responses (of agreement or disagreement) to the statement: "This community (or area) is really a separate community (or area) from Nashville and should have a separate government."

TABLE VIII-A

Relationship between Suspicion[a] of the Central City among Voters outside the City and Opposition to Reorganization

Vote	Per cent	
	Suspicious	Not suspicious
For reorganization	35.3	79.5
Against reorganization	64.7	20.5
N(=100%)	34	39
$X^2 = 12.89$, df $= 1$, p $< .001$		

a. As measured by responses (of agreement or disagreement) to the statement: "On the whole, big city politics are more corrupt than smaller city politics."

TABLE VIII-B

Relationship between Suspicion[a] of the Central City among Voters
outside the City and Opposition to Reorganization

| | Per cent | |
Vote	Suspicious	Not suspicious
For reorganization	37.5	75.0
Against reorganization	62.5	25.0
N(=100%)	32	40
$X^2 = 8.80$, df $= 1$, p $< .01$		

a. As measured by responses (of agreement or disagreement) to the statement: "As a rule, it is better to live in small communities with small governments than large communities with large governments."

that the first question was a little stronger than the next two, thus detecting only the extraordinarily "suspicious" who would be all the more likely to oppose reorganization. It is also possible that the second two questions, because of their more abstract, less personal and less immediate nature, elicited agreement from many people who were not really hostile to the City of Nashville as such, whereas those who agreed to the first question, which is both concrete and immediate, tended to be hard-core "hostiles."

Additional interview data relevant to this hypothesis may be seen by categorizing the respondents according to residence, as living in the old city, the recently annexed area, in a suburban city, in a rural area, and in an unincorporated suburban area. Compared with the respondents' answers on how they voted, these data are presented in Table IX. The reader should understand that no claim is made that this is a procedure for measuring "suspicion" of the central city among fringe dwellers. It was nonetheless hoped that this approach would serve to indicate more precisely the areas of fringe opposition.

The frequency distributions in Table IX do not tell us a great deal because all categories of respondents outside the city supported reorganization (except "rural" which split in half), although by a lesser total percentage than city respondents. Thus if the fringe dwellers interviewed *were* suspicious of the central

TABLE IX

Relationship between Place of Residence and Expressed Opposition to Reorganization:
Interview Sample

Vote	Within city			Outside city			
	Old city	Annexed area	Totals	Sub-urban city	Rural area	Unincorporated Suburban area	Total
For reorganization (per cent)	63.8	89.2	73.7	66.7	50.0	57.7	57.5
Against reorganization (per cent)	36.2	10.8	26.3	33.3	50.0	42.3	42.5
N (= 100%)	58	37	95	9	12	52	73

$X^2 = 14.85$, df $= 4$, p. $< .01$

city (and there is no measure of this here) a majority of them did not show their suspicion by opposing reorganization, or else they gave the interviewer an incorrect answer when asked whether they voted for or against Metro. It is also possible that a great proportion of "yes" voters were interviewed because they were more co-operative (fewer refusals) and easier to find than "no" voters.

In the actual vote, of course, the old city, the county rural areas, and the suburban cities, taken as a whole, all voted against the charter. The actual voting figures rounded to the nearest percentage point are presented in Table X.

A comparison of the sample percentages and the percentages in the actual vote (Tables IX and X) shows that in every geographic area but one (unincorporated suburban areas) the sample percentages are very unlike the actual percentages. No doubt the discrepancy is due in part to the *ex post facto* nature of the interviewing, with a resulting bias on the pro-Metro side. It is probably true also that "no" voters were more reluctant to co-operate in view of the Metro victory. Most of the un-co-operative respondents were, in fact, in the old city, an area where the sample percentage was not even close and where there were a lot of Ben West supporters. In addition, six respondents in the old city claimed that they had not voted at all, even though their cards indicated that they had. Fraudulent voting practice is a possibility here, especially in the light of postconsolidation scandals in Nashville.

In the rural and suburban city areas the sample percentages were different from the actual percentages. In fact, both rural and suburban city areas voted "no," but in the author's sample the rural respondents split 50–50, while suburban city respondents voted "yes." In the unincorporated suburban areas, however, the sample percentage was quite close (which perhaps in large measure accounts for the closeness of the total county percentage). It is also worth noting that the number of interviews

TABLE X

Relationship between Geographic Area, by Groups of Precincts, and the 1962 Metro Vote

	Per cent						
	Within city			Outside city			
Vote	Old city	Annexed area	Totals	Suburban city	Rural area	Unincorporated suburban area	Totals
For reorganization	45.2	72.2	57.4	47.3	34.0	62.6	56.0
Against reorganization	54.8	27.8	42.6	52.7	66.0	37.4	44.0
Totals (= 100%)	19,960	16,726	36,686	19,706	4,040	4,040	28,408

NOTE: The author's grouping of "rural" and "unincorporated suburbs" precincts is explained below. The number of precincts in each group is also given.

in the rural area and in the suburban cities was very small, 12 and 9 respectively, whereas the number interviewed in unincorporated suburban areas was 52.

Voter Ignorance and Unfamiliarity with Local Government. The hypothesis tested here is that less knowledgeable voters are more likely to oppose reorganization than more knowledgeable ones.

Among the measures of voter knowledgeability used in Nashville were two fixed-alternative questions designed to test the respondents' familiarity with the proposed consolidation charter. They were asked to pick from a card those answers which expressed what they thought would happen to the six suburban cities under Metro. Would they be abolished or permitted to decide for themselves whether to join the new government? And could places in Davidson County other than the suburban cities be annexed under Metro against the will of the people concerned? The correct answer to the first question is "permitted to decide for themselves" and to the second question the correct answer is "can be annexed even if the people don't vote for it."

The data from these questions, compared with responses on how the respondents voted, are presented in Tables XI and XI-A.

TABLE XI

Relationship between Voter Ignorance[a] of a Reorganization Proposal and Opposition to Reorganization

| | Per cent | |
| | Answering | Not answering |
Vote	correctly	correctly
For reorganization	73.1	50
Against reorganization	26.0	50
N (= 100%)	104	26
$X^2 = 4.12$, df $= 1$, p $< .05$		

a. As measured by responses to the question: "The six suburban cities (Belle Meade, Berry Hill, Oak Hill, Forest Hills, Goodlettsville, Dupontonia) will be (1) abolished, (2) permitted to decide for themselves."

TABLE XI-A

Relationship between Voter Ignorance[a] of a Reorganization
Proposal and Opposition to Reorganization

| | Per cent | |
| | Answering | Not answering |
Vote	correctly	correctly
For reorganization	50	81.7
Against reorganization	50	18.3
N (= 100%)	54	71
$X^2 = 17.12$, df $= 1$, p $< .001$		

a. As measured by responses to the question: "Other places in Davidson County, besides the surburban cities mentioned above (1) cannot be annexed, (2) can be annexed only if the people vote for it, (3) can be annexed even if the people don't vote for it."

The data in these two tables are in conflict as to their support for the hypothesis. In the first table the less knowledgeable voters split evenly, whereas the more knowledgeable voters strongly supported the reorganization proposal. Thus although the less knowledgeable did not oppose the reorganization, they did vote against it proportionately more than the knowledgeable voters. This supports the hypothesis as stated.

In the second table, however, the less knowledgeable voters heavily supported the proposal and the more knowledgeable voters split evenly. The hypothesis, of course, predicted that the former were more likely to oppose reorganization than the latter. The data in this table, therefore, offer nothing in the way of confirming the hypothesis.

It is possible to explain the large number of respondents answering the second question incorrectly in that the heavy stress laid by Metro's proponents on the evils of annexation under the existing structure misled many voters into believing that under Metro involuntary annexation would be impossible. Perhaps many of them voted for Metro precisely on these grounds. This "explanation" is plausible, but there are no data to support it.

Another measure of voter ignorance (or understanding) was an open-ended question asking the respondents what courses of action other than Metro might metropolitan areas take to deal with some of their problems. Answers were coded by the author as either "knowledgeable" or "unknowledgeable." Answers regarded as knowledgeable included annexation by the central city, partial consolidation, and intergovernmental co-operation. Unknowledgeable answers included "make studies," more civic spirit by the citizenry, better leadership, and the levying of higher city taxes. The results, compared with the way respondents voted, are presented in Table XII.

TABLE XII

Relationship between Voter Ignorance[a] and Opposition to Reorganization

| | Per cent | |
| | Knowledgeable | Unknowledgeable |
Vote	answers	answers
For reorganization	86.2	63.6
Against reorganization	13.8	36.4
N = (100%)	29	140
$X^2 = 4.62$, df $= 1$, p $< .05$		

a. As measured by responses to the question: "What courses of action, other than Metro might metropolitan areas take in your view?

Of those whose answers were knowledgeable (to a fairly stiff question) an overwhelming 86.2 per cent supported reorganization. The less knowledgeable also supported it, but in less striking fashion. Thus these data provide support for the hypothesis.

A final test for the hypothesis compared education, measured by last grade in school, with voting. It is not claimed that this procedure provides a measure of ignorance about government as such; it merely indicates the general educational level of the respondent. The results are presented in Table XIII.

TABLE XIII

Relationship of Voter Education Level to Opposition
to Reorganization

Vote	Grades 1–8	Grades 9–11	Per cent High school graduate	Some College	College Graduate
For reor- ganization	33.3	57.7	71.4	80.8	95.7
Against reor- ganization	66.7	42.3	28.6	19.2	4.3
N(=100%)	30	26	63	26	23
$X^2 = 25.36$, df $= 4$, p $< .001$					

Respondents in the grade school category were the only group to oppose Nashville's consolidation. All other groups supported Metro in a very clear pattern of increasing support with increasing education and decreasing support with decreasing education. Stated another way, the data show that the fewer the number of years in school the greater the opposition. Clearly this is some support for the hypothesis, although the measure used (years in school) is not an accurate measure of knowledge about government.[7]

The author also considered the possibility that this correlation is as much "income" as "education." If this were true, of course, the poorly educated voters (anti-Metro) would be predominantly the same persons as those in the very low-income brackets. By the same token the well-educated voters would be predominantly the same persons as those in the very high-income brackets.

Table XIV shows the support for Metro at each intersection of the two stratified populations. For example, 38.5 per cent of those with eight grades or less of education and under $3,000 yearly income voted for Metro. Since the pro-Metro percentages generally increase across the rows and not down the columns—

7. Such a striking correlation of higher formal education and greater support for Metro may be related in part to the strong support of teachers in the 1962 campaign.

that is, the percentages increase with increasing education—these data suggest that education was a more relevant variable than income.

This is shown more clearly by summing row and column inversions. An "inversion" refers, for example, to the fact that if income were the most relevant variable one would expect a percentage increase from one cell to the next down each *column*, showing that support increases with increasing income. Similar increases from cell to cell could be expected across each *row* if education were the most relevant variable. Using this procedure here reveals but three inversions in the rows and eight in the column, thus showing a more regular relationship between in-

TABLE XIV

Relationship of Income to Education Level

Reported Annual income under	Support for Metro (Per cent)				
	Grades 1–8	Grades 9–11	High school graduate	Some college	College graduate
	(n=13)	(n=3)	(n=1)	(n=2)	(n=1)
$3,000	38.5	66.7	100	100	100
3,000–	(n=9)	(n=10)	(n=20)	(n=3)	(n=5)
5,999	33.3	60.0	70.0	66.7	100
6,000–	(n=3)	(n=10)	(n=23)	(n=12)	(n=7)
9,999	66.7	50.0	60.9	75.0	100
10,000–	(n=4)	(n=3)	(n=7)	(n=6)	(n=6)
14,999	0.0	66.7	57.1	83.3	83.3
15,000–	(n=1)	(n=0)	(n=4)	(n=3)	(n=4)
and over	0.0	. . . .	100	100	100

Note: Column and row totals are not relevant here. The relevant totals are those in each cell. The percentages show what part of that total voted for Metro.

creasing education and support for reorganization than between income and such support.

In any case the income categories used in this study were probably too broad to permit any very meaningful conclusions as to whether it is "really" low income or low education that is correlated with opposition to metropolitan government. For

Rows	Number of inversions	Columns	Number of inversions
1	0	1	1
2	1	2	2
3	1	3	3
4	1	4	1
5	0	5	1
Total =	3	Total =	8

example, the category $3,000 to $5,999 would seem to cover both the very poor and the fairly well off.

No consistent pattern emerges from all these data on voter knowledgeability and opposition to governmental reorganization. It therefore seems possible to conclude from the sample data that voter ignorance (at least of government) and *opposition* are not significantly associated, perhaps because ignorance is manipulatable and can go either way. On the other hand, the sample data do suggest that voter support is associated with greater knowledge about local government and with higher education.

SUMMARY OF RESULTS

Hypothesis One. The sample data showed greater support for reorganization among voters not satisfied with services than among those satisfied; that is, 81.1 per cent of the former voted "yes," whereas 52.6 per cent of the latter voted "yes." The sample data thus support the hypothesis as stated. As is obvious, however, even among those expressing satisfaction a majority voted for the proposal.

Hypothesis Two. The sample data showed that a majority of voters who indicated that they anticipated higher taxes with reorganization voted against it, whereas those who did not anticipate higher taxes voted for it. The sample data therefore fully confirm the hypothesis.

The possibility was also considered that this correlation represents as much the satisfaction or dissatisfaction with services variable as the anticipation or nonanticipation of higher taxes. The resulting frequency distributions lent some support to this hunch, but the anticipation of higher taxes variable still appeared to be relevant. Thus even while holding the services variable constant there was still greater opposition to reorganization among voters anticipating higher taxes than among those not anticipating higher taxes. Consequently the hypothesis was not rejected.

Hypothesis Three. From all three measures of "suspicion" the sample data showed opposition to reorganization among outside voters who expressed suspicion of the central city and support among outside voters who did not express suspicion. The sample data therefore support the hypothesis.

Hypothesis Four. From the first two measures of ignorance (and knowledgeability) the sample data were in conflict regarding support for the hypothesis. In neither case did the ignorant, or the less knowledgeable, *oppose* reorganization, but in the first case they did vote against it proportionately more than the knowledgeable voters. The second measure, however, resulted in the less knowledgeable heavily *supporting* reorganization.

From the third measure of voter ignorance the data showed greater opposition among the less knowledgeable than among the more knowledgeable, although a majority of both groups voted for reorganization.

Thus the first and third measures provide support for the hypothesis as worded.

From the final measure (one of general education level only) the sample data showed that the fewer the number of years in school the more the opposition. The author also considered the possibility that this correlation is as much "income" as "education." The resulting frequency distribution provided no confirmation of this hunch.

Taking all the measures together, the picture is thus, a mixed one with only partial support for the fourth hypothesis. The sample data do suggest, however, that a "yes" vote is associated with greater knowledge about local government and especially with higher education.

ANALYSIS OF THE AGGREGATE VOTE

The Geographic Variable. It was noted above in connection with voter-attitude hypothesis three (county suspicion of the city and its government) that the actual voting figures would bear on this question. What then do the voting data indicate about the support or opposition of different geographic areas?

To begin with, it is necessary to remember that Metro passed in Nashville and Davidson County in 1962. Therefore both central city and county outside supported the proposed consolidation, by 57 per cent and 56 per cent margins respectively. (See Table XV.) A breakdown of the aggregate figures, however, reveals some important geographic variations. Thus when the central city is divided into old city and annexed area the results are striking. And when the county outside is then broken down by groups of precincts into incorporated, unincorporated, and rural places[8] further important variations appear. (See Table XVI.)

TABLE XV

Vote on the 1962 Metro Charter, by City of Nashville
and County Outside

Vote	Nashville	County outside	Total
For	21,064 (57.4%)	15,897 (56.0%)	36,961 (56.8%)
Against	15,622 (42.6)	12,511 (44.0%)	28,133 (43.2%)
Total	36,686 (100%)	28,408 (100%)	65,094 (100%)

Source: For and against figures supplied by the Metropolitan Nashville Election Commission. Totals represent arithmetic totals of for and against votes. See Table XX, p. 151, for all the figures by Nashville ward and Davidson County civil district (Table XX is in the section entitled "Additional Tables").

A number of plausible explanations for these figures may be suggested. In the old city it appears that Mayor West's political machine carried the day. The reader will recall that the old city voted the Mayor's position in 1958 as well; he was then for consolidation. The only city wards that voted "yes" in 1962 were

8. The classification of precincts as rural or suburban was difficult in some cases. A few of the choices made were perhaps arbitrary, based on the writer's experience in the area. In most cases, however, precincts were clearly rural in character.

TABLE XVI

Relationship between Geographic Area, by Groups of Precincts, and 1962 Metro Vote

	Within city			Outside city			
	Old city	Annexed area	Total	Unincorporated suburban area	Rural area	Incorporated Sub-urban cities	Total
Number of Precincts	42	27	69	53	20	6	79
Vote							
For reorganization	45.2	72.2	57.4	62.6	34.0	47.3	56.0
Against reorganization	54.8	27.8	42.6	37.4	66.0	52.7	44.0
Numbers of voters (= 100%)	19,960	16,726	36,686	19,706	4,040	4,662	28,408

the third and fourth. These two wards contain both the major non-Negro universities and the majority of higher-income city voters. The fourth ward, the highest income ward in the city, heavily supported Metro on both occasions.

In the *recently annexed areas* it is possible that antiannexation, anticity, and anti-Ben West sentiments, whether clearly separated by the voters or not, resulted in an overwhelming (72 per cent) pro-Metro vote.

Interestingly enough, these same annexed-area precincts also voted for Metro in 1958 by about 54 per cent,[9] perhaps because their residents feared or disliked the prospect of annexation. In any case, the annexed area carried the central city for Metro in 1962.

In the county it appears that the *unincorporated suburban areas* played a part comparable to that of the annexed areas in the city; that is, they pushed the entire area into the "yes" column. The heavy vote of the unincorporated suburbs—particularly Donelson, Inglewood, Hillwood, and Crieve Hall—carried the county for consolidation. In 1958 Donelson and Inglewood—both heavily populated areas—voted overwhelmingly against the proposal. Madison and the Maplewood district voted against it both times.

Turning to *incorporated places* in the county, it is interesting that the three high-income cities (Belle Meade, Oak Hill, and Forest Hills) all voted for Metro—by 54 per cent, 57 per cent, and 69 per cent respectively. They also supported Metro in 1958 by even higher margins. In 1962, however, Dupontonia, Goodlettsville, and Berry Hill all opposed Metro by margins of 76 per cent, 77 per cent, and 68 per cent.

It is quite possible that the higher education levels in the upper-income suburbs, plus their perhaps less locally oriented populations, was the deciding factor. Goodlettsville, Dupontonia (Lakewood), and Berry Hill all opposed Metro. Goodlettsville and

9. The exact percentage could not be computed from the planning commission figures because one precinct that appeared in the annexed area in 1962 could not be located among the precincts listed for 1958.

Dupontonia, of course, are several miles from the city of Nashville and represent long-established settlements. Such places are not likely to look very favorably on "being taken into the city."

Nearly every rural precinct in the county opposed Metro in 1962. Farmers and rural homeowners are also likely, of course, to view city-county consolidation in terms of the city reaching out to get them.

The Racial Variable.   Another important variable is the racial one. What do the voting data indicate about the support or opposition of Negroes compared with whites?

In a recent study of Negro political leadership in Nashville, Boardman Stewart determined the percentage of nonwhites in each of the city's forty-two precincts. Inasmuch as census tract boundaries do not coincide with precinct boundaries in Nashville, this was almost a Herculean task. Briefly, Stewart's procedure was to fit the census data (white and nonwhite), presented block by block in terms of census tracts, into the precincts. This in turn involved a good deal of field work to determine exact boundaries. His procedure disclosed that thirteen precincts, all in the old City of Nashville, had a majority of "nonwhites." The per cent of nonwhites varied from 57.9 to 98.9.[10] The vote in these precincts (using planning commission data) compared with that in the remainder of the precincts in the old city, is presented in Table XVII.

Only two precincts with a nonwhite majority supported Metro. Both were in the councilmanic district of Z. Alexander Looby, a long-time supporter of the proposal. In striking contrast, the three precincts in Councilman Robert Lillard's district returned pro-Metro votes of only 32, 21, and 39 per cent.

The reader will recall that a majority of Negro voters also voted against consolidation in 1958. Only one of Looby's precincts was in the yes column in 1958, and none of Lillard's was. It seems plausible, therefore, that the idea associated with the

10. H. Boardman Stewart, "A Study of Negro Political Leadership in Nashville" (unpublished research paper, Department of Political Science, Vanderbilt University, 1962).

TABLE XVII

Relationship between Race, by Groups of Precincts,
and 1962 Metro Vote

| | Per cent | |
	White	Nonwhite
Number of precincts	29	13
Vote		
For consolidation	45.4	43.2
Against consolidation	55.6	56.8
Number of voters (= 100%)	14,438	5,298

more traditional Negro politicians—that Metro meant a dilution of their city-centered voting strength—reached large numbers of Negroes. Another factor was perhaps the low educational level of Negroes, making more difficult an understanding of such a complex issue as city-county consolidation.

Of course the white voters in the old city also voted against Metro, although it is unlikely that they did so because they wished to thwart its dilution of the Negroes' city-centered voting power. Nonetheless, both whites and nonwhites in the old city voted against Metro, and by very similar percentages. While the data thus provide little evidence that the racial factor was of great importance, it is quite possible that whites and Negroes voted similarly for quite different reasons: the whites in support of Ben West and the Negroes in fear of their voting power.

POSSIBLE CRITICAL FACTORS IN THE NASHVILLE EXPERIENCE

The question considered in this section is that of possible critical factors in the Nashville "success story." The purpose here is to consider certain factors advanced by observers of the Nashville scene as "critical." Such conclusions may well be subjective, but they may also be insightful. At the very least, they are possible sources of hypotheses for subsequent studies.

Although Nashville's success story would perhaps never have been written without the grass-roots promotional campaign of the Citizens Committee for Better Government and the exceptional aid and support of the Nashville *Tennessean*, it is the view of a number of observers in the Nashville area that these last two forces would have been ineffective without the large annexation in 1960.

It is, of course, frequently assumed that a major impediment to governmental reorganization in a metropolitan area is the tension between central city and county outside. In Nashville in 1958 the county defeated Metro, but four years later the county area supported it. What happened in the intervening years to bring about such a change of heart?

When the twenty-one key observers were asked this question, the response was unanimous—"annexation and the green sticker." This, it seemed to many, made it possible for the proponents of change, led by the crusading *Tennessean*, to stigmatize successfully the status quo and to champion Metro as a device for eliminating not only these two evils but also the fomentors of the evils —Ben West and the city administration. "The overwhelming vote on June 28 was made possible not because of the merits of Metro but because people assumed they were eliminating annexation, the green sticker, and the city administration."[11] In these words, Joe Torrence summed up the view of many observers, although most laid special stress on annexation.

The animosity generated by annexation and the sticker, moreover, was probably felt most keenly in the very two geographic areas that swung the referendum to Metro—the recently annexed area and in the unincorporated suburbs which seemingly, or allegedly, were next in line for annexation.

The suggestion is therefore made by most of the key observers that the anticity vote in 1962 was a pro-Metro vote and that the support of the majority of county residents would not have been forthcoming except for certain anticity attitudes.

The reader will recall, however, that the sample data presented in the first section of this chapter indicated that those who were "suspicious" of the city, according to the three measures used,

11. Interview with Joe Torrence, Financial Director, City of Nashville, November 29, 1962.

opposed consolidation. The anticity respondents were "no" voters.

There is thus a clear contradiction between the sample data and the conclusion of the key observers. How can this be explained? There are, of course, many possibilities. The sample may have been off, the questionnaire measures of suspicion may have uncovered only the extraordinarily "suspicious" who would not vote for governmental integration under any circumstances, and the twenty-one key observers may have been wrong. There is, however, a kind of corroboration for the latter's interpretation in the sample data from the following two open-ended questions. If the sample is suspect these data are of course also suspect, but there is no question here of the validity of a measure (although there is the problem of the accuracy of the author's coding procedure). In any case, the following is presented in the interest of a complete disclosure of results. All respondents (not just those outside the city) were asked, "Why did the people vote for Metro this time and against it last time?" All respondents were also asked, "What was the most important reason causing *you* to vote for (or against) Metro?" The results of these questions, coded by the author and broken down geographically, are presented in Tables XVIII and XIX on pages 149, 150 in the section entitled "Additional Tables."

The basic assumption governing the use of these two questions was that they would be an indication of the way the respondents themselves felt. Regarding the second question, it was assumed that some respondents would express idealized or "acceptable" reasons in order to appear reasonable and intelligent to the interviewer. Regarding the first question, it was not assumed that this would uncover the actual reasons for the people's support in 1962. On the other hand, responses to a question about "the people" are some indication of the attitudes of individual voters.

Table XVIII indicates that the most frequently-cited reasons for other people's support for Metro were fear or dislike of annexation and dislike of the mayor and/or the city. Both of these reasons probably related to the cluster of attitudes associated with annexation and the "green sticker," although the latter is not specifically included. The reason the green sticker is not included is that it was seldom mentioned by the respondents. (The responses presented in the tables repeat as closely as possible the words of the respondents.) This of course casts some doubt on the worth of the key observers' conclusions, at least in regard to this one issue.

The reader will also note that a much higher percentage of respondents selected these two reasons in the "crucial areas" (the annexed area and the unincorporated suburbs) than in other areas. Combining the two answers in each of the "crucial" areas the resulting percentages are 61 per cent (annexed areas) and 67 per cent (unincorporated suburbs).

Somewhat different results were obtained from the question, "What was the most important reason causing you to vote for Metro?" (See Table XIX.) The most frequently-cited reason in this case was "consolidation and resulting efficiency or lower cost." When broken down geographically, moreover, this was still the most popular reason in the old city and the crucial annexed area. In the unincorporated suburbs (the second crucial area) "fear and dislike of annexation" was the most popular reason (29 per cent), whereas "better services" and "consolidation and resulting efficiency" received 24 per cent of the responses.

It is possible, however, that the discrepancies in responses to the questions, "Why did the people vote for Metro this time?" and "Why did you vote for Metro?" reflect a reluctance on the part of some voters either to admit that they were impelled by negative motives (such as dislike of the mayor or of annexation) or failure to recognize that they were.

It is also possible that had there been no annexation or crudely imposed wheel tax in the period between referenda the Nashville consolidation could not have been accomplished. It is certainly true, in any case, that the circumstances that pertained to Nashville from 1958 to 1962 have not been common to proposals for governmental reorganization in metropolitan areas.

10

GENERAL CONCLUSIONS

THE outcome in Nashville of a proposal for metropolitan integration was not the usual one. Therefore voter attitudes underlying support for integration—and other evidence about the sources of such support—are perhaps the most important findings of this study. The Nashville interview data suggest that voter support for metropolitan integration is associated with dissatisfaction with public services, the nonanticipation of higher taxes stemming from integration, education levels higher than grade school, and an understanding of "metropolitan problems."

A common-sense conclusion from the aggregate voting data, in addition, is that annexation transformed the usual "no" vote of fringe residents, an anti-city vote, into a "yes" vote. The relevant interview data, however, contradict this conclusion. In fact, the interview data suggest that anticity fringe residents were "no" voters, whereas the common-sense conclusion from the aggregate voting data (widely shared by the key observers) suggests that anticity fringe residents were "yes" voters. The latter were presumably "yes" voters because they preferred Metro to being annexed by Mayor West's city government.

It is interesting to note in this connection that all three of Virginia's city-county consolidations since 1950 took place in an atmosphere of fear of annexation. All three involved the merger of a metropolitan county and a small city; all three were initiated by county officials; and all three were stimulated, at least in part, by county fear of annexation by the central city. Thus the consolidation of Phoebus, Hampton, and Elizabeth City County in 1952 was stimulated by fear of Newport News' annexation intentions. Similarly, South Norfolk and Norfolk County, and Virginia Beach and Princess Anne County—both in 1963—were stimulated by fears of Portsmouth and Norfolk.[1]

Obviously the three Virginia consolidations are not perfectly comparable with Nashville's—they did not involve merger with a central city, for example—but in all four cases the fear of annexation was present, and all four succeeded where so many have failed.

More research doubtless is needed into the character and correlates of fringe "suspicion" of central cities.

Unlike many attempted reorganizations, in any case, the Nashville experience can be viewed as offering fringe residents a choice between two departures from the status quo: annexation or consolidation. For Nashville's fringe residents the choice was not simply between an innovation and a familiar status quo. Of course, one can also view the Nashville experience as offering a choice between an innovation and a status quo that had become unbearable to many people. Evidently many central city voters supported Metro for such reasons. A great many fringe residents, however, showed considerable awareness of—and fear of—the prospect of annexation. (See Table XVIII.)

After viewing several attempts at metropolitan integration, especially those in Miami, Cleveland, and St. Louis, Scott Greer has suggested that the available alternatives for bringing about metropolitan reform are to manipulate the electorate through redefining (or misdefining) the issue and to bring about change through fiat. The former course, he finds, was taken in Dade County, and the latter in Toronto.[2] The Nashville experience would seem to fall into the Dade County category. Surely the

1. See David O. Temple, "Merger in Virginia Local Government," *University of Virginia News Letter,* XL, No. 2.

2. Scott Greer, *Metropolitics: A Study of Political Culture* (New York: John Wiley and Sons, 1963), p. 199.

annexation of 85,000 county residents before the 1962 referendum helped Metro's proponents put the issue on a personal, barely relevant basis, namely, for or against Ben West. The insertion of a "devil," moreover, simplified the task of selling a highly complicated consolidation charter. It is certainly true, in any case, that the circumstances which pertained to Nashville from 1958 to 1962 have not been common to proposals for metropolitan integration. This in turn lends some support to Robert C. Wood's hypothesis that "program expansion of urban governments" not initiated from without the system, nor by highly mobilized elite groups, is random—"the result of accident, not design."[3]

If Nashville's consolidation is in fact random and the result of accident, not design, it offers little reason for optimism to those who would like to "find out how it's done" from the Nashville experience. Whether the Nashville experience is grounds for unmitigated pessimism on the part of reformers may also be questioned, if only because such sources of voter support as dissatisfaction with services, higher education levels, and some kind of apprehension over annexation are liable to be present in other areas. It is the conclusion here, however, that Nashville's success story is *sui generis*.

Perhaps those sociologists and political scientists are correct who contend that governmental integration runs counter to the very nature of the metropolitan community. The present study is not the place to explore this concept in detail,[4] but basically the

3. Robert C. Wood, "The Contribution of Political Science to Urban Form," in *Urban Life and Form,* ed. Warner Z. Hirsch (New York: Holt, Rinehart and Winston, 1963), p. 113.

4. For an elaboration of this conceptual scheme see Edward C. Banfield and James Q. Wilson, *City Politics* (Cambridge: Joint Center for Urban Studies of M.I.T. and Harvard University, 1963), esp. Chaps. 2 and 3, and Oliver P. Williams *et al.,* "Urban Differentiation and the Governing of Metropolitan Areas," in *Suburban Differences and Metropolitan Policies: A Philadelphia Story* (Philadelphia: University of Pennsylvania Press, 1965). See also Scott Greer, *Governing the Metropolis* (New York: John Wiley and Sons, 1962), pp. 23–41 and Eshref Shevky and Wendell Bell, *Social Area Analysis* (Stanford: Stanford University Press, 1955).

argument is that "urbanization" or "metropolitanization" are the equivalent of the heavy concentration in a few square miles of people with different income, occupational, educational, cultural, ethnic, and racial characteristics. These diverse social and economic characteristics become *spatially distributed* in the metropolitan area; that is, one sub-area may contain Negroes, another upper-income whites, another college-educated people, and so on.

To carry the argument one step further, it is held that governmental integration, although perhaps recommended by the fact of economic interdependence among metropolitan subareas, flies directly in the face of the natural tendency of these diverse communities and neighborhoods to try to maintain their separateness, which is grounded in actual differences.

The various communities tend to verbalize their separatist efforts, moreover, in such terms as "grass-roots government," or "government close to the people," and in so doing they lay claim to a great American tradition.[5] The success of this appeal to tradition in the interest of separatism is reflected both in the fragmented structure of government in metropolitan areas and in the repeated failure of reorganization attempts. It would seem, moreover, that the Nashville experience, although a success story to warm the hearts of reformers everywhere, does little to upset the utility of this conceptual scheme.

5. See Robert C. Wood, *Surburbia: Its People and Their Politics* (Boston: Houghton Mifflin, 1959).

EPILOGUE

T HE successful referendum on June 28, 1962, did not, of course, usher in a completely mature consolidated government. Several problems and hurdles still remained, and the most serious of these was the pending court decision on the constitutionality of the new form of government.

It will be recalled that this legal challenge[1] rested on the following grounds: that there had been an unconstitutional delegation of legislative power to the charter commission; that the charter attempted to authorize taxation which would not be equal and uniform throughout the territorial jurisdiction of the government, in violation of constitutional requirements; that Amendment Eight to the constitution did not authorize consolidation of cities and counties and the creation of an entirely new form of government; and that the terms of office of the appellant, Ben West, and of all the officers and officials of Nashville were unconstitutionally abridged by the metropolitan charter.

1. The suit was brought under a declaratory judgment statute. Complainants were Mayor Sam Davis Bell of Belle Meade, Lewis Frazier, former commissioner of Forest Hills, and Robert Lillard. Mayor West was named as a defendant and joined the complainants in contesting Metro's constitutionality. The Metro charter commission was allowed to intervene as defendants supporting the validity of the charter. Their briefs were filed by Edwin Hunt, legal counsel for the commission.
2. This complaint recalls the words of John A. Rush: "It seems difficult for them (some judges) to realize that this new form of government is an entirely new political entity clothed with power to perform the functions of both a city and a county." John A. Rush, *The City-County Consolidation* (Los Angeles: By the author, 1941), p. 302.

141

In early July preliminary arguments were heard in Nashville Chancery Court by Chancellor Glenn W. Woodlee of Dayton, Tennessee. On July 17 the Chancellor took the case under advisement and while so doing halted all transitional moves to the new form of government, except the election of metropolitan mayor scheduled for November 6, 1962.

On August 4, Chancellor Woodlee announced his decision upholding the constitutionality of the consolidation. Rejecting all the complainants' arguments, the Chancellor used language that could not but please anyone who advocated governmental integration in metropolitan areas. In disposing of the complaint that there had been an improper delegation of legislative power, Woodlee said:

> We are not here concerned with the rigidness of Article II, Sec. 3, and the limited delegation of power thereunder, because we are not considering that which was written in 1796, 1834, and 1870 but the Eighth Amendment to the Constitution which was adopted . . . July 1953.

He went on to note that the Eighth Amendment authorized the General Assembly to provide for the consolidation of any or all functions of municipal corporations and counties. This, he said, the General Assembly did by means of the Enabling Act of 1957 and subsequent private legislation. The Chancellor then injected a lengthy quotation from a *Vanderbilt Law Review* article citing the serious problems stemming from "the growth of urban population beyond the legal boundaries of our towns and cities," problems which, the article continued, "are not being handled effectively by existing agencies of local government." The quotation went on to note the annexation was often an impractical solution to such problems.

> This brings us to a crucial problem. . . . Our Amendment [Eight] makes no mention of a new third unit to which both city and county functions may be transferred. It must be interpreted to permit such consolidations, however, unless we are to make the unreasonable assumption that those who gave us this Amendment contemplated transfers of "any or all" functions of great metropolitan cities to county government designed to handle only es-

sentially rural affairs. Surely it is generally understood that consolidation, if not exclusively, is primarily a metropolitan area concern.

As to the constitutional "requirement" that taxes be equal and uniform, the Chancellor said this:

> To hold that the local taxes must be equal and uniform throughout Davidson County, including the urban area, would have the practical effect of rendering inoperative the consolidation of all city functions with county functions provided by the Eighth Amendment. This interpretation must necessarily have such crippling effect upon "the consolidation of functions" as to render meaningless . . . this Amendment.

Finally, Chancellor Woodlee spoke directly to those who would construe so strictly the constitution and the general laws as to preclude such governmental innovations as city-county consolidation.

> To those members who have opposed changes in Tennessee's basic law, let me express a final word. I respect their convictions, but we live in a world of change, and changes come whether we will them or not. . . . Let us open another gate to future development and progress in popular government in Tennessee, and give the people abundant opportunity to improve on what we have.[3]

On October 4, 1962, the Supreme Court of Tennessee handed down a ruling sustaining the opinion of the lower court. Again all the complainant's arguments were rejected, and the following significant language was added:

> Too much importance cannot be placed upon the fact that Constitutional Amendment No. 8 was approved by a vote of the people, as was every step taken during the development of this Amendment No. 9. And each election was a mandate of that proposed Amendment No. 8.

> .   .   .   .

> And, after all, this is the people's government. Their wishes, constitutionally expressed, must prevail, no matter how much it upsets the previous status quo.

---

3. *Lewis Frazier et al.* v. *Joe C. Carr et al.* The text of the opinion by Chancellor Woodlee is reproduced in August 7, 1962, Nashville *Tennessean.*

With the constitutional barrier out of the way at last, the elections for metropolitan mayor, vice mayor, and council were held November 6 and November 27. Beverly Briley defeated Clifford Allen for Mayor (the vote was 58,333 to 34,466);[4] and George Cate, Jr., was elected vice mayor over H. Sanders Anglea. The new council of 40 persons was elected, with 35 from districts and 5 at large.

Nevertheless, weighty problems of transition, not least of which were the inflated hopes for Metro generated by its more enthusiastic proponents, faced the metropolitan government of Nashville as it entered its first year.

4. The Nashville *Tennessean,* November 7, 1962.

ADDITIONAL TABLES

BIBLIOGRAPHY

INDEX

ADDITIONAL TABLES

TABLE II

Population of Davidson County Communities
and Census Divisions,
1960

	1960
Donelson	16,381
Oak Hill (incorporated)	4,490
Goodlettsville division and city (city incorporated)	3,163
Inglewood	26,527
Madison	13,583
Maplewood division	9,173
Nashville South division	27,262
Belle Meade (incorporated)	3,082
Woodmont–Green Hills–Glendale	22,159
Nashville Southeast division	21,481
Forest Hills (incorporated)	2,101
Berry Hill (incorporated)	1,551
Woodbine–Radnor–Glencliff	14,485
Old Hickory division	7,123
Dupontonia city (now Lakewood, incorporated)	1,896
West Meade–Hillwood division	9,788

Source: Adapted from U. S. Bureau of the Census, United States *Census of Population: 1960. Tennessee*, Vol. I.

TABLE III

Vote on 1958 Metro Charter By Nashville Wards
and Davidson County Civil Districts

Nashville Ward	Per cent for	Per cent voting	Total vote
1	40.9	15.2	987
2	44.8	14.1	746
3	65.7	22.3	1775
4	78.2	34.1	3793
5	50.7	18.6	2144
6	52.6	19.8	1186
7	61.5	23.7	1969
Total	61.9	22.2	12,605

County "civil district"	Per cent for	Per cent voting	Total vote
2	21.3	45.5	1131
3	31.9	44.0	3013
4	17.5	47.2	1891
5	21.7	42.3	539
6	35.3	40.4	3836
7	72.3	50.4	4585
8	53.6	40.8	2600
9	12.0	47.5	332
10	9.3	50.8	1210
11	26.1	40.4	2155
12	24.9	34.8	1748
13	20.9	37.6	728
14	6.9	45.9	596
15	44.4	44.7	4742
16	67.1	45.9	3923
Total	41.8	43.8	33,029
Grand Total	47.3	34.5	45,634

Source: Daniel J. Elazar, *A Case Study of Failure in Attempted Metropolitan Integration: Nashville and Davidson County, Tennessee* (Chicago: National Opinion Research Center of the University of Chicago, 1961), p. 3.

TABLE XVIII

Responses to the Question: "Why Did the People Vote for Metro this Time and Against It Last Time?"

Responses	Per cent						
	Within city			Outside city			
	Old city	annexed area	Totals	Sub-urban city	rural area	Unincorporated suburban area	Totals
Fear, dislike of annexation: prefer Metro	9.1	34.2	20.7	12.5	20.0	43.5	35.9
Dislike of mayor and/or city	27.3	26.3	26.8	25.0	30.0	23.9	25.0
People understood better, better explained	27.3	15.8	21.9	37.5	20.0	6.5	12.5
To improve things: no specifics	9.1	7.9	8.5	...	...	4.3	3.1
Consolidation and resulting efficiency or lower cost	9.1	7.9	8.5	...	...	2.2	1.6
The vote of other people or sections	...	2.6	1.2	12.5	10.0	6.5	7.8
To get better services	11.4	2.6	1.2	...	10.0	8.7	1.6
To handle growth problems	2.3	...	3.7	...	...	2.2	4.7
Other	4.5	2.6	7.3	12.5	10.0	2.2	7.8
Totals (= 100%)	58	37	95	9	12	52	73

TABLE XIX
Responses to the Question: "What Was The Most Important Reason Causing You To Vote for Metro?"

Per cent

Responses	Within city			Outside city			
	Old city	Annexed area	Totals	Suburban city	Rural area	Unincorporated suburban area	Totals
Consolidation and resulting efficiency or lower cost	47.1	54.5	50.7	50.0	33.3	23.7	22.2
To improve things generally: no specific	26.5	3.0	14.9	…	…	5.3	3.2
Better services	11.8	15.2	13.4	16.7	50.0	23.7	20.6
Dislike of mayor and/or city	8.8	21.2	14.9	…	16.7	10.5	7.9
To handle growth problem	5.9	…	2.9	33.3	…	…	7.9
Fear, dislike of annexation: prefer Metro	…	6.1	2.9	…	…	7.9	17.5
Totals (=100%)	58	37	95	9	12	52	73

TABLE XX

Vote on the 1962 Metro Charter by Nashville Wards
and Davidson County Civil Districts

County District	Per cent For	Per cent Voting	Total Vote
2	37.5	40.3	674
3	69.2	45.1	4065
4	35.6	49.7	2245
5	57.2	45.7	1141
6	68.2	44.4	2527
7	59.1	54.6	2383
8	71.2	52.7	2205
9	32.8	47.6	393
10	24.7	45.8	1399
11	47.9	37.4	2521
12	57.7	35.7	1859
13	38.7	41.9	1231
14	31.0	44.5	693
15	66.7	44.3	3543
16	56.6	54.4	1529
County Totals	55.9	43.9	28,408

Nashville Wards	Per cent For	Per cent Voting	Total Vote
1	32.9	31.9	2246
2	24.9	31.4	1784
3	50.7	37.7	2825
4	62.4	39.0	4490
5	42.2	31.9	4079
6	38.3	26.9	1649
7	42.3	33.7	2887
Totals 1-7	45.1	33.7	19,960
8	64.4	40.6	4533
9	79.2	50.2	8953
10	63.6	41.5	3240
Totals 8-10	72.2	45.3	16,726
Totals City	57.4	38.1	36,686
Grand Totals	56.8	40.4	65,094

SELECTED BIBLIOGRAPHY

Adrian, Charles R. *Governing Urban America*. New York: McGraw Hill, 1961.

————. *Public Attitudes and Metropolitan Decision Making*. Pittsburgh: Institute of Local Government, University of Pittsburgh, 1962.

————. "Metropology: Folklore and Field Research," *Public Administration Review*, XXI, No. 3 (Summer 1961), 148–156.

Advisory Commission on Intergovernmental Relations. *Factors Affecting Voter Reactions to Governmental Reorganization in Metropolitan Areas*. Washington, 1962.

————. *Governmental Structure, Organization, and Planning in Metropolitan Areas*. Washington, 1961.

Banfield, Edward C. *Political Influence*. New York: The Free Press, 1961.

Bollens, John C. (ed.) *Exploring the Metropolitan Community*. Berkeley: University of California Press, 1961.

———— et al. *Metropolitan Challenge*. Dayton, Ohio: Metropolitan Community Studies Incorporated, 1959.

———— and Henry J. Schmandt, *The Metropolis*. New York: Harper and Row, 1965.

Booth, David A. *Metropolitics: The Nashville Consolidation*. East Lansing: Institute for Community Development and Services, Michigan State University, 1963.

Briley, Beverly. "Keynote Address Before the Urban County Congress, National Association of County Officials." New York, March 15, 1959.

Community Services Commission for Davidson County and the City of Nashville. *A Future For Nashville: Summary of Findings and Recommendations*. Nashville, 1952.

153

Editors of *Fortune. The Exploding Metropolis.* Garden City, New Jersey: Doubleday, 1958.

Elazar, Daniel J. *A Case Study of Failure in Attempted Metropolitan Integration: Nashville and Davidson County, Tennessee.* Chicago: National Opinion Research Center, The University of Chicago, 1961.

Fiser, Webb S. *Mastery of the Metropolis.* Englewood Cliffs, New Jersey: Prentice Hall, 1962.

Government Affairs Foundation. *Metropolitan Surveys: A Digest.* Chicago: International City Manager's Association, 1958.

Grant, Daniel R. "Urban and Suburban Nashville: A Case Study in Metropolitanism," *Journal of Politics,* XVII (February 1955), 82–99.

―――, and Lee S. Greene, "Surveys, Dust, Action," *National Civic Review,* L (October 1961), 466–471.

Greer, Scott. *Governing the Metropolis.* New York: John Wiley and Sons, 1962.

―――. *Metropolitics: A Study of Political Culture.* New York: John Wiley and Sons, 1963.

Gulick, Luther. *Metropolitan Problem and American Ideas.* New York: Alfred A Knopf, 1962.

Havard, William C. and Floyd L. Corty, *Rural-Urban Consolidation.* Baton Rouge: Louisiana State University Press, 1964.

Jackson, Donald W. "Taxpayers Look at Consolidated Government." Speech Before the Memphis Rotary Club, Memphis, October 9, 1962.

Long, Norton E., "Recent Theories and Problems of Local Government," in Carl J. Friedrich and Seymour E. Harris (eds.), *Public Policy.* Cambridge: Graduate School of Public Administration, 1958.

McDill, Edward, and Jeanne Clare Ridley, "Status, Anomia, Political Alienation, and Political Participation," *American Journal of Sociology,* LXVII (September 1962), 205–213.

Metropolitan Government Charter Commission. *Proposed Metropolitan Government Charter for Nashville and Davidson County,* Nashville: Citizens Committee for Better Government, 1958.

Municipal Year Book 1962. Chicago: International City Managers' Association, 1962.

Ostrom, Vincent, et al., "The Organization of Government in Metropolitan Areas," *American Political Science Review,* LV, No. 4 (December 1961), 831–842.

Presthus, Robert. *Men at the Top.* New York: Oxford University Press, 1964.

Proposed Charter of the Metropolitan Government of Nashville and Davidson County, Tennessee. Nashville: Metropolitan Government Charter Commission, 1962.

Robson, W. A. (ed.) *Great Cities of the World: Their Government, Politics, and Planning.* London: Allen and Unwin, 1954.

Rush, John A. *The City-County Consolidated.* Los Angeles: By the Author, 1941.

Schmandt, Henry J., *et al. Metropolitan Reform in St. Louis: A Case Study.* New York: Holt, Rinehart and Winston, 1961.

Sengstock, Frank S. *et al., Consolidation: Building a Bridge Between City and Suburb.* St. Louis: St. Louis University School of Law, 1964.

Sofen, Edward. *A Report on Politics in Greater Miami.* Cambridge: Joint Center for Urban Studies of MIT and Harvard University, 1961.

"The Future Metropolis," *Daedalus,* XC No. 1 (Winter, 1961).

U. S. Bureau of the Census. *Census of Governments: 1962. Governmental Organization,* Vol. I.

———. *United States Census of Population: 1960. Tennessee,* Vol. I.

———. *United States Census of Population: 1960. Tennessee, General Population Characteristics,* Vol. I.

———. *United States Census of Population: 1960. United States Summary,* Vol. I.

West, Ben. "Statement to the Davidson County Delegation." Nashville, January 11, 1961.

Zimmer, Basil G. and Amos Hawley, "Local Government as Viewed by Fringe Area Residents," *Rural Sociology,* 23:363–370, December 1958.

PERSONAL INTERVIEWS

Nashville Interest Group Leaders, Politicians, and Other Observers

Name	*Status*	*Date Interviewed*
Clifford Allen	County Tax Assessor, former State Senator, candidate for first Metropolitan Mayor	November 29, 1962
Thomas J. Anderson	John Birch Society Leader, Editor of *Farm and Ranch*	November 29, 1962
Dick Battle	Local politics reporter, the Nashville *Banner*	December 13, 1962
Beverly Briley	County Judge, first Metropolitan Mayor	December 19, 1962
Dr. James Dunning	President, Goodlettsville Area Chamber of Commerce	November 30, 1962
Amon Carter Evans	Publisher, The Nashville *Tennessean*	November 26, 1962
A. D. Gillem	Nashville City Councilman, Mayor West's Floor Leader	December 22, 1962
Professor Vivian Henderson	Economics Professor, Fisk University	December 17, 1962
Robert Horton	Director of Research, Nashville–Davidson County Planning Commissions	November 11, 1962
Edwin F. Hunt	Legal Counsel, 1958 and 1962 Charter Commissions	December 14, 1962

Name	*Status*	*Date Interviewed*
Donald W. Jackson	Executive Secretary, Tennessee Tax-payer's Association	December 3, 1962
Mrs. Gus Kuhn	President, Nashville League of Women Voters	November 11, 1962
Robert Lillard	Nashville City Councilman	December 3, 1962
Matthew Lynch	Secretary, Tennessee State Labor Council	December 18, 1962
Clarence McIntyre	Administrative Assistant to Mayor West	December 18, 1962
Dr. James M. Phythyon	Chairman, Projects Committee, Civic Committee on Public Education	November 28, 1962
James H. Roberson	Co-ordinator, Citizens' Committee for Better Government	December 18, 1962
Mrs. J. D. Sanders	Chairman, Women's Division, Citizens' Committee for Better Government	December 1, 1962
John H. Stambaugh	Vice-Chancellor, Vanderbilt University, member of the Nashville Area Chamber of Commerce	November 20, 1962
Joe Torrence	Finance Director, City of Nashville, member 1962 Charter Commission	November 29, 1912
Ben West	Mayor, City of Nashville	November 29, 1962

INDEX

Adrian, Charles R., 14–16, 25–26
Advance Planning and Research Division of the Joint City and County Planning Commission, 38–39, 44, 98
Albuquerque, New Mexico, 25
Allen, Clifford, 24, 47, 65, 81n, 88, 91, 97–98, 103n, 104, 144. *See also* Davidson County Tax Assessor
Anderson, Thomas J., 91, 101–102, 102n
Anglea, H. Sanders, 91, 99, 144
Annexation, as a device for metropolitan integration, 9, 10–11; in Nashville, 36–37, 39–40, 45, 58–67, 69, 80–82, 86, 105, 108, 134–136; in Tennessee, 36–37, 37n, 68

Bainbridge, Glenn, 98
Baker v. *Carr*, 21
Banfield, Edward C., 8n, 106–107, 107n, 139n
Barrett, George, 95
Baton Rouge, Louisiana, 9n, 25
Battle, Dick, 61, 62n, 103n
Bell, Sam Davis, 77, 141n
Bogen, Robert, 73, 96
Bollens, John C., 7n, 27, 28n, 31n
Booth, David A., 51n, 90n, 106n
Bramwell, Charles, 60n, 63
Branstetter, Cecil, 71–72, 96
Briley, Beverly, in defense of suburbanites, 22, 22n; as County Judge, 24, 68; preferred consoli-

dation, 39–40; role in legislative action, 42; supported by *Tennessean*, 62n; and annexation, 65–66; campaign for Metro mayor, 47, 144; and charter commission, 72–77; role in 1962 Metro campaign, 88, 91, 97–98, 104, 106. *See also* Davidson County Judge
Buffalo *Courier Express*, 5

Carr, Joe C., 77, 143n
Cate, George, Jr., 88, 91, 93, 96–97, 144
Charter Commission, 1958, 41, 43–46, 52, 68, 81n, 99
Charter Commission, 1962, 66–67, 68–78, 81n, 84, 89, 91, 93, 96
Chenault, R. N., 71–74
Citizens' Committee, 1958, 47–48
Citizens' Committee for Better Government (CCBG), 1962, 52n, 71, 73, 73n, 81n; and 1962 Metro campaign strategy, 79–80, 83, 83n; role in 1962 campaign, 91–99, 104n, 106–107, 133
Civic Committee on Public Education, 52n, 73, 90, 93, 95–96
Cleveland, Ohio, 25, 138
Clouse, Ewing, 43, 69
Cochran, Carmack, 71–72, 96
Community Services Commission for Davidson County and the City of Nashville, 35–38, 42, 63, 68
Cornwell, Glenn, 99
Council of Jewish Women, 91, 93, 96

159